PRAISE FOR *LIMITLESS LIFE*

"My friend Derwin Gray graciously opens the doors for all and invites us to courageously remove labels, step out of the world of judgment and self-condemnation and into the abundant, fulfilling, limitless life God has planned for us all."

— Marshall Faulk, pro football Hall of Fame inductee and Super Bowl champion

"Derwin Gray writes like a madman on a mission—a mission to trumpet the truth about who we really are in spite of the labels and lies some have succumbed to. Full of biblical insight and wisdom, *Limitless Life* offers answers for living the limitless life in Christ."

— Judah Smith, pastor, City Church; author, *Jesus Is*

"Derwin is one of the great young preachers in America. God has given him the ability to teach the Gospel in a practical and powerful way. As you read this book, God will stretch the limits of your life. You'll never be the same again!"

— Rick Warren, founding pastor, Saddleback Church; author, *The Purpose Driven Life*

"If there is anyone who can speak authentically about living life to your fullest God-given potential, it's my friend Derwin Gray. As a pastor, dad, husband, and author, I've witnessed him overcome unbelievable obstacles from his past. As a friend and brother, I know the tenderness with which he cares for people. This book will lead you forward, challenge you to move, and pastor you on the journey."

— Clayton King, president, Crossroads Ministries; teaching pastor, NewSpring Church; campus pastor, Liberty University

"No one can deny the limiting effect sin has on our lives, but God calls us to die to that sin and embrace the limitless love expressed through his son. In this helpful book, Derwin Gray paints a picture of that grace, and calls us step out in faith and to live truly limitless lives."

— Ed Stetzer, author, *Subversive Kingdom*; www.EdStetzer.com

"Absolutely phenomenal. I read it all in one sitting while on a plane. I couldn't put it down! Growing up with so many false labels put on me—unloved, fatherless, etc.—*Limitless Life* was water to my soul. Buy two copies! One for you and one for a friend. You won't finish reading this book unchanged."

— Jefferson Bethke, author,
Jesus > Religion

"Derwin is the real deal. He's authentic and provides much needed permission to all of us to get real as well. He knows what it's like to feel like a nobody—and reveals how you're a somebody truly loved by God with the opportunity for limitless life."

— Brad Lomenick, president, Catalyst;
author, *The Catalyst Leader*

"*Remember* Jesus' statement that he came to give us life to the fullest? Derwin Gray explains what a life without limits really looks like and gives practical steps to make that a reality."

— Craig Gross, founder, xxxchurch.com;
author, *Open: What Happens When
You Get Real, Get Honest, and Get
Accountable*

"*Limitless Life* will help you understand life's challenges in the context of God's sovereignty and the incredible story he is telling through your life. You don't need to live a life of fear, regret, and defeat any longer. Child of God. Beautiful. Valued. Precious. Worth dying for. Loved by Jesus. *Limitless Life* will remind you these are titles that can now define you!"

— Brian Dodd, tribal leader of
The Rocket Company; www
.BrianDoddOnLeadership.com

"In Derwin Gray's marvelous *Limitless Life* you will find a book permeated and soaked—marinated—in God's grace, but in this book you will discover that grace doesn't stop with forgiveness and acceptance, great as those gifts are, but with the transforming power of the God who wants to make you the person God designed you to be. The message of this book is that God finds you where you are and in his gracious love picks you up and takes you home where you can find a new identity and a new life. This book explodes from the heart of a man whose life has been trans-formed and from a church marked by transformation. Buy this book and then buy a second copy for your best friend. This book can start a transformation revolution."

— Scot McKnight, Professor of New
Testament, Northern Seminary,
Lombard, Illinois; author of *The Jesus
Creed* and *The King Jesus Gospel*

LIMITLESS
LIFE

*You Are More Than Your Past
When God Holds Your Future*

BY DERWIN L. GRAY

THOMAS NELSON
Since 1798

NASHVILLE   DALLAS   MEXICO CITY   RIO DE JANEIRO

Published in Nashville, Tennessee, by Thomas Nelson. Thomas Nelson is a trademark of Thomas Nelson, Inc.

Published in association with the literary agency of Fedd & Company, Inc., Post Office Box 341973, Austin, TX 78734.

Thomas Nelson, Inc., titles may be purchased in bulk for educational, business, fund-raising, or sales promotional use. For information, please e-mail SpecialMarkets@ThomasNelson.com.

Unless otherwise indicated, Scripture quotations are taken from THE ENGLISH STANDARD VERSION. © 2001 by Crossway Bibles, a division of Good News Publishers.

Scripture quotations marked GNT are taken from THE GOOD NEWS TRANSLATION. © 1976, 1992 by The American Bible Society. Used by permission. All rights reserved. Scripture quotations marked GW are taken from the GOD'S WORD TRANSLATION. Copyright © 1995 by God's Word to the Nations. Used by permission of Baker Publishing Group. Scripture quotations marked HCSB are taken from the HOLMAN CHRISTIAN STANDARD BIBLE. © 1999, 2000, 2002, 2003 by Broadman and Holman Publishers. All rights reserved. Scripture quotations marked KJV are taken from the King James Version (public domain). Scripture quotations marked MSG are taken from *The Message* by Eugene H. Peterson. © 1993, 1994, 1995, 1996, 2000. Used by permission of NavPress Publishing Group. All rights reserved. Scripture quotations marked NCV are taken from the New Century Version®. © 2005 by Thomas Nelson, Inc. Used by permission. All rights reserved. Scripture quotations marked NLT are taken from the *Holy Bible*, New Living Translation. © 1996, 2004, 2007. Used by permission of Tyndale House Publishers, Inc., Carol Stream, Illinois 60188. All rights reserved.

Library of Congress Cataloging-in-Publication Data

Gray, Derwin L., 1971–
  Limitless life : you are more than your past when God holds your future / by Derwin L. Gray.
     pages cm
  Includes bibliographical references.
  ISBN 978-1-4002-0536-3
  1. Christian life. I. Title.
  BV4501.3.G7358 2013
  248.4—dc23   2013003824

Printed in the United States of America

14 15 16 17 RRD 6 5 4 3

Transformers, on February 7, 2010, we set out together on a great adventure with nothing but God the Father, God the Son, and God the Holy Spirit; God's vision for Transformation Church—and each other. Since that time, God has taken our breath away! I dedicate *Limitless Life* to you. Other than being a beloved child of God, husband to Vicki, and father to Presley and Jeremiah, I have no greater honor or joy than serving you as your lead pastor. Thank you for the privilege. Oh yeah, strap on your spiritual seat belts: God is just getting started with us! Upward, inward, outward, Transformers—roll out!

CONTENTS

FOREWORD

AS HUMAN BEINGS, WE ARE NAMERS BY NATURE. THE BOOK OF GENESIS tells us that Adam named the animals. We haven't stopped, have we? We label everything. Even people. Even ourselves.

In some ways this is good. Labels separate things; they establish limits. We need this. It was, after all, by naming the animals that Adam realized he was different and required a different companion. And think about all the areas of life where we depend on labels: Our maps. Our businesses. Our food. Ask a pharmacist: a bad label is the difference between medicine and poison.

The trouble is that there are a lot of bad labels floating around. Because people are namers by nature, we give and pick up a lot of labels, and a lot of them are bad news. They might be from sins in our past, failures in our present, the pins and jabs people tagged us with growing up. Wherever they come from, they are limiting our lives.

If things are mislabeled they create unhelpful boundaries, false limitations. If you label yourself a failure, you limit your chances for success. If you label yourself as weak, you limit your strength. If you label yourself a disappointment, you limit your ability to see that people appreciate you—or that God appreciates you.

My friend, Derwin Gray, is all about helping people lose the negative labels holding them back and showing them the new labels that God wants to use to move them forward. He has his own experience with destructive labels, and as the pastor of Transformation Church he's been working with others to overcome their own. He calls them "soul-tattoos," those indelible marks that are imprinted on our hearts and limit us.

Derwin shows us what's possible for us if we move from afraid to courageous; from addict to free; from mess to masterpiece; from orphan to adopted; from damaged goods to trophy of grace; from religious to grace-covered; from consumer to contributor; from purposeless to purposeful; from worker to worshiper; and from failure to faithful.

How does it happen? When Jesus becomes our new label. When he tears off the old markers and imprints his life on and in ours. With Christ our identity makes a radical transformation and the things that held us back become the steps we walk on our journey with Jesus. If you're looking for the limitless life, this is the place to start. If you're looking to get free, Derwin points the way.

Mark Batterson
April 2013

INTRODUCTION

DEAR READER,

I'm Derwin. I'm an ordinary guy who has battled against destructive labels for a lifetime. Many of us are stuck believing the negative messages that come from these kinds of labels because they are often stitched on our hearts at an early age, and this has limited our lives. Labels can be difficult to shed because, for better or worse, they can become our identity, and it is difficult to let go of that.

WHAT IS A LABEL?

A label is a soul-tattoo that is ingrained deep in our hearts, so much so that it determines how we see ourselves. And how we see ourselves determines how we live.

A false label leads to living a lie. And a life built on a lie places you in a spiritual prison. Jesus wants to give you, free of charge, labels that are true. And His labels will set you free (John 8:32).

A destructive label leads to living a destructive life. There is soul-thief, a dark enemy that wants to nail ruinous labels to your heart so he can steal your life. Jesus wants to give you life-giving labels that release your potential for the good of the world. He said, "The thief comes only in order to steal, kill, and destroy. I have come in order that you might have life—life in all its fullness" (John 10:10 GNT).

We are going to journey through ten chapters together. But we will not be traveling alone. Supernaturally, we will be on this journey with Jesus. At each and every step, He will lead and move us into a deeper discovery of who He is and what He has accomplished for us so we can reach our potential by embracing new labels that He personally tattoos on our hearts. But don't worry: Jesus' ink never grows dim or dull. The more you believe in Him and the labels He has given you, the brighter the colors of these new labels become. We begin to see ourselves as His Father sees us. And when that happens, everything changes. Life becomes *limitless*.

The message of *Limitless Life* will utterly transform you.

You will become more courageous and take greater risks.

You will accomplish things you didn't even know you were allowed to dream about.

You will be set free from destructive habits that once harmed and limited you.

You will experience and see yourself in a whole new light that will cause you to shine like the stars in the sky.

You will forgive people you never thought you would forgive.

You will love those you thought you would forever hate.

You will live a life that, when you've breathed your last breath, will leave the world better because you existed.

My heart skips a beat at the thought of seeing your life become a canvas God uses to display His beautiful artwork for the world to admire.

I recommend that you read *Limitless Life* with a community of friends, perhaps your small group or Sunday school class or an online community. This way you have a shared learning experience with others on the same journey. There is power in community.

At the end of every chapter, there is a "Transformation Moment" consisting of three sections: "Head," "Heart," and "Hands." The Head section deals with a big idea from the chapter. I want you to use that idea to wallpaper your mind. And please feel free to think of your own big idea in the chapter that you want to integrate into your life.

The Heart section is a prayer I want you to pray. As we journey together, you will find you have labels that can only be removed by the power of prayer. Prayer is basically saying, "Jesus, I need You to do this in my life. I can't, but I know You can."

The Hands section is a call to action; true learning only happens as we practice what we are learning. The more you practice what you learn from each chapter, the more stunning and life-transformative things will take place. You will break free from the labels that are holding you back. And you will enter a new land called Limitless.

SO, WHERE ARE WE GOING?

As we journey to a land called Limitless, we are going to replace negative labels that limit our lives, such as "Afraid" or "Addicted," with new labels that release our God-given potential, such as "Courageous" and "Free." It isn't enough to remove old, hurtful labels. We must write new labels on our hearts to begin infusing positive messages.

WHAT WILL *LIMITLESS LIFE* ACCOMPLISH IN YOUR LIFE?

Negative labels are thieves that steal your destiny and imprison you in a life of mediocrity.

The life-giving labels that Jesus imparts give you permission to expect Him to do epic things through your life. "God can do anything, you know—far more than you could ever imagine or guess or request in your wildest dreams! He does it not by pushing us around but by working within us, his Spirit deeply and gently within us" (Eph. 3:20 MSG).

Today is the day you go get that "far more than you could ever imagine or guess or request" kind of life that God is calling you to experience. This is the essence of living a life without limits. Today is the day you break free from the labels that have limited you. God has a limitless life that awaits you. Let's go get it. I'm honored to journey with you.

ONE

FROM AFRAID TO COURAGEOUS

I learned that courage was not the absence of fear, but the triumph over it. The brave man is not he who does not feel afraid, but he who conquers that fear.[1]

—Nelson Mandela

PICTURE A BATTLEFIELD. THE PHILISTINES HAVE GATHERED THEIR ARMY for battle on one side of the mountain; the Israelites are gathered on the other. Between the two armies lies a valley.

But there is far more than a valley separating Israel from victory. Yes, a giant named Goliath—a seasoned, undefeated champion—towers over them.

And yet, something even more dangerous than the indomitable giant stands in their way. What could possibly strike more fear in their hearts than this unconquered foe? A message that evokes insecurity, an even more insurmountable opponent—the label stitched in Israel's heart: "Afraid." Its message has been ingrained so deeply that fear has paralyzed them and robbed them of the ability to seize their destiny.

In the days of ancient Israel, wars were sometimes settled when the two champions from rival armies fought to the death. The victor and his people would then enslave their opponents. For forty days, Goliath demanded that an Israelite fight him, but none stepped up. No man from Israel had the courage to enter the valley and fight on behalf of his nation. Not a single one was willing to defend God's honor.

For a while it appeared that fear had won the day. Each Israeli soldier had surrendered his destiny because he'd accepted the "Afraid" label and allowed it to produce such fear in him that even living as a slave became an acceptable alternative to taking up arms.

Then God sent David.

DAVID WAS DIFFERENT

The daily routine of Goliath's challenge to Israel and their refusal to rise to the occasion continued—until one day, when a boy named David arrived on the scene. The lad showed up believing his assignment was to see how his brothers, soldiers in Israel's army, were doing. Little did David know that God had a plan in sending him. The God of Israel was getting ready to rewrite history.

As David was checking on his brothers, the teenager heard Goliath challenge the armies of the living God. These taunts pierced David's heart, and he was stunned that no man from the nation of Israel would accept Goliath's challenge.

But David was different. Though limited by size, experience, and strength, he accepted the giant's invitation to battle.

Goliath seemed superior to David on all fronts, so why did the teen respond to the call? What made David think he would fare any better than every man in Israel's army? He responded because he was courageous. Instead of allowing the label "Afraid" to define him, he permitted the life-giving label "Courageous" to guide him. David knew who he was and whose he was, and therefore he knew how to be courageous. David had a firm grasp on his identity as a child of God, and it was his faith in that label that enabled him to act—and history was changed.

The "Afraid" label produces fear. And fear is a thief that steals the courage of far too many, paralyzing and imprisoning them in a life of mediocrity. I've not only seen it, I have experienced it. My story is tattooed with "Afraid." Perhaps yours is too.

FEAR OF REJECTION

My dad was nineteen when I was born. By the time I was six, he was pretty much out of my life. I only saw him from time to time after that. My precious mom was seventeen, just a baby herself, when she gave birth to me. Yet for one so young, her heart was already deeply wounded due to the many destructive labels painfully stitched into it. The damage they'd inflicted was an ongoing struggle in her life, so my grandmother primarily raised me, and my grandfather provided for my physical needs.

As a little guy, I really couldn't process what was going on in my family. I just knew that Dad was not around and that Mom was in and out of my life. In my little child's mind, I understood that certain people who should have been close to me were not consistently around, though I didn't know why.

As early as I can remember, an "Afraid" label in my heart produced a fear of rejection. And it limited me.

Just like the Israelites, I was paralyzed by "Afraid." I couldn't fight for my destiny because fear stood in the way. By the time I reached my early twenties, that label had become so firmly affixed to my heart that I feared every relationship I had would end with rejection. I was consumed with thoughts such as, *Why let anyone get close to me when ultimately they will leave me?* I intentionally kept people at a distance. My heart was in a steel cage, and I wouldn't let anyone have the key.

FEAR OF NOT BEING "GOOD ENOUGH"

The "Afraid" label also produces the fear of not being good enough. It certainly did for me. Despite my success as an NFL player, I never felt I measured up—in anything.

That fear started when I was about nine and tried out for my first football team. I still remember the coach calling out the names of the players who made the cut. As he called out each one, I waited to hear my name, but I never did.

One of the coaches approached me, and I remember trying my best to hold back the tears as he said, "You've got to come back next year. You were not good enough this year." With that, the fear of never being good enough began lodging itself in my heart. I wish just one person had told me, "Derwin, your value as a human is not in making a football team. You are valuable because God purchased your life with the life of His Son."

Although I did not make the first team I tried out for, I developed an insatiable work ethic from the experience. It propelled me to work hard as a high school football player for the legendary coach D. W. Rutledge, at Converse Judson

High School in Converse, Texas. We won the 1988 state championship, and I was named first team all-state. Later I was the recipient of a Division I scholarship to Brigham Young University (BYU).

Despite this success, however, the "Afraid" label already had been firmly embedded in my soul. I was still afraid I was not good enough. I learned that even earthly success couldn't strip away negative labels. No matter how successful I was, I remained crushed under the weight of fear. This continued to plague me as a college football player at Brigham Young, and later in the NFL.

The Israelites were crushed by this same fear. All they could see was Goliath's size and reputation. They could not understand, as David did, the strength that would be theirs through their faith.

FEAR OF NOT BEING SMART ENOUGH

Ever felt dumb? For much of my life, I did. Yet I'm one of the only men in my family to graduate from high school or college.

As a child, I was pretty much on my own with my homework. My grandmother only had a sixth-grade education, and no one else was around to help. Additionally, I had a severe stuttering problem and did not dare ask questions in class. Who wants to be laughed at? In tenth grade, I took French, and for one of the tests, everyone had to stand in front of the class and speak in French. Because of my stuttering, I just couldn't do it. Mercifully, the teacher let me make my presentation after class. With those significant obstacles in my way, school was an ongoing struggle, and I labeled myself as "dumb."

Throughout high school and college, I took classes I knew

I could pass with ease in order to stay eligible for football. I didn't challenge myself in school. I took the easy road, all because I thought I was dumb.

The irony is that today I have a master's degree with honors (magna cum laude), and a radio show that reaches about 350,000 people per week. I've worked for ESPNU and FOX TV in Charlotte, North Carolina, as a football analyst, and I'm a pastor. None of these accomplishments fits with the "dumb" perception I had of myself. None could have been realized if I had continued to wear the "Afraid" label. I allowed that label to rob me of so much in my youth, unlike David, who did not allow his youth or the label his people wore to stand in the way of doing what he knew was right.

FEAR OF THE UNKNOWN

At BYU, I met Vicki, a striking javelin thrower. She became my girlfriend in the winter of 1990, and my wife on May 23, 1992. She was twenty-two, and I was just twenty-one when we got married.

Neither Vicki nor I went to church. We hadn't a clue who Jesus was or how His love had the power to transform lives. What we did know was that we were afraid. Vicki's parents had gotten a divorce when she was five. And the first wedding I'd ever attended was my own!

My bride and I had no idea how our labels would negatively affect us after saying, "I do." My fear of rejection would limit my ability to let her love me and would cause me to withhold love from her. At the same time, her fear of being discovered as imperfect would limit her ability both to love me and to receive love from me.

The Israelites encountered this same type of limiting fear.

They cowered in their tents, allowing Goliath to mock their God and demean their people on a daily basis. But David waded into the unknown, trusting that the God in whom he had full faith would equip and protect him in defeating this enemy.

God has a stunning vision for your life, but if He showed it to you all at once, it would be too much to handle. In His grace, He gives small glimpses at a time, and His unimaginable vision for your life can only unfold as you have the courage, like David, to move into the unknown. But when the "Afraid" label is sewn into our hearts, we fear the unknown. This fear holds us back from seizing our destinies and accomplishing what God has called and created us to accomplish.

FEAR OF FAILURE

I'm often asked if I miss playing in the NFL. I always say, "No!" The reason is that for five of my six years in the NFL, I did not enjoy football because of soul-crushing fear.

As a little boy, my dream was to play in the National Football League. On April 25, 1993, that dream became a reality when the Indianapolis Colts drafted me. But I spent every day waiting for the coaches to tell me I was not good enough anymore, that I was no longer needed on the team. I lived in fear that they would fire me. And if I got fired, who would I be if not an NFL player? I'd be a nobody. And this thought made it impossible to enjoy living out my dream.

On June 17, 1996, my wife gave birth to Presley, our daughter. The first moment Presley's big brown eyes caught mine, she had my heart. I've been in love with that girl ever since. But immediately after she captured my heart, all kinds of thoughts ran through my mind: *What kind of dad will I be? I never had a dad. Who is going to teach me to father her? Can I protect her from guys like I used to be?*

Then, on August 22, 2000, my son, Jeremiah, arrived on the scene. Again, more fear and questions. Even though I was a Christ-follower by that time, that old "Afraid" label continued to limit me.

Today I am the lead pastor of an incredible church called Transformation Church. This was not on my agenda in any way when I was attending college. In fact, starting a church and becoming a pastor were *never* on my list of goals. But God had other plans.

I was in one of my seminary classes, working through the book of Ephesians, when God very clearly impressed on my heart: *Start a church. Call it Transformation Church, because I transform lives. I want it to reflect My heart and be multiethnic.*

I wasn't just afraid. I was terrified. How could someone who didn't grow up in church *start* one? How could a stutterer get up and speak to people on a regular basis? And I had struggled through school. How could I teach others?

Only God knows how many dreams have been killed at the altar of fear. It must break His heart to see dreams He has placed in so many people's hearts go unrealized because we have more faith in fear than in Him. But in a world with so many "Goliaths," how *can* we be fearless like David?

TIME FOR A NEW LABEL

We have looked at some of the many fears that can be produced by the "Afraid" labels in our hearts. Now it's time to begin replacing those labels with a new one: "Courageous."

Let's walk through some keys to *courage* that will begin to wipe out fear's limiting message in your heart.

Key 1: Have a Humble Heart

At one point in Israel's history, God rejected the reigning king, Saul. The man just couldn't obey God, not even to save his life. (You can read about his shenanigans in 1 Samuel 15.) When God gave the prophet Samuel the assignment of finding the next king of Israel, He led Samuel to Jesse's home.

Jesse had several impressive-looking sons, and Samuel probably thought choosing a king from among them would be simple, a no-brainer—but God didn't want any of them to be king. He wanted the boy who stood among the smelly sheep, David. Why? Because David was humble. God only stitches new labels in the hearts of those who are humble enough to admit they need new ones.

We have a tendency to go after the Goliaths, seeking glory, before spending the time learning how to humbly serve where God wants us. Yet, before David stood ready to fight Goliath in the valley, he had stood in a different valley, taking care of a dirty, stinky flock. Before he defeated the great giant, he had humbly allowed God to shape his character while he had the seemingly insignificant task of tending some animals.

Many great, epic displays of God's glory through His children are built on hours, even years, of performing an unnoticeable, seemingly unimportant task. It was in the valley of sheep that God made humble David into "a man of valor." There God imprinted the label "Courageous" on David's heart, transforming a lowly boy into "a man of war" as he honed his skills at warding off lions and bears, and preparing him to defend what He would one day entrust to his care. While David wore a shepherd's garb, God was making him "a man of good presence" (1 Sam. 16:15), one who gained dignity as he took responsibility for his family in the absence of his brothers.

In the valley of sheep, David learned to depend on God. God's presence, provision, and power accompanied David wherever he went, and people could see it. This set him on the path to defeating Goliath. But in fact, because of his time alone with God, David had defeated Goliath before the battle even started. Muhammad Ali, perhaps the greatest boxer to ever live, was right when he said, "The fight is won or lost far away from witnesses—behind the lines, in the gym and out there on the road, long before I dance under those lights."[2]

Maybe you're in your own valley of sheep right now. Maybe you think you are going unnoticed and your assignment is not what you want it to be. Just remember, we must go through the valley, where we humble ourselves before God, before we can go out for God and bring Him glory by slaying a Goliath. You glorify God, too, by being faithful in the small things.

Many people never get to slay a Goliath because they think that taking care of sheep is beneath them. This is pride, and God resists the proud but generously gives grace to the humble (James 4:6).

Key 2: Believe That God and His Love for You Are Bigger Than Your Giant

Fear caused the men in Israel's army to think that the giant was bigger than God. But David took Goliath's challenge because he knew God was bigger than the giant. When God stitches the "Courageous" label in your heart, giants seem small in comparison to Him. You will find yourself attempting things for God's glory that make no sense to most people. The odds will be stacked against you, but courage moves us to trust God, who is greater than any odds, to act on our behalf so He will be made famous through us.

Never forget this: fear paralyzes us from acting on behalf of God's glory, but faith mobilizes us to live courageously for God's glory. And David had faith that God loved him.

My children, Presley and Jeremiah, know that I love them. They trust me. And because of that, courage surges through them because they know Daddy has their backs. When we know God loves us, we trust Him. Do you know that God loves you?

I'm not asking if you simply know that as a theological fact. I'm asking if you have experienced God's love as the apostle Paul describes:

> I pray that from his glorious, unlimited resources he will empower you with inner strength through his Spirit. Then Christ will make his home in your hearts as you trust in him. Your roots will grow down into God's love and keep you strong. And may you have the power to understand, as all God's people should, how wide, how long, how high, and how deep his love is. May you experience the love of Christ, though it is too great to understand fully. Then you will be made complete with all the fullness of life and power that comes from God. (Eph. 3:16–19 NLT)

Like David, when we know God loves us, we can trust Him when we face the giants of life. The Philistine giant didn't intimidate David because David knew God's love for him was bigger than Goliath. The giant didn't limit David's life because the God without limits propelled David to victory. You can face your giants and win too.

Dr. Martin Luther King Jr. beautifully said it takes "dikes of courage to hold back the flood of fear."[3] Jesus is the builder.

11

And He's ready, willing, and able to build dikes of courage in your heart so you can have a limitless life.

Key 3: Expect Opposition . . . and Use It as Fuel

As David questioned the Israeli soldiers about Goliath and what would be given to whoever killed him, his brother Eliab scolded him. Check out 1 Samuel 17:28: "Now Eliab his eldest brother heard when he spoke to the men. And Eliab's anger was kindled against David, and he said, 'Why have you come down? And with whom have you left those few sheep in the wilderness?'"

This is why I love the Bible—it cuts to the very heart of humanity. Here is the older brother, who instead of fighting for God's glory was paralyzed by fear. His "Afraid" label rendered him a coward, and then he did what cowards do. He attacked the courageous David, forbidding him to even ask questions, let alone fulfill his destiny.

Just as with David, people close to you will discourage you from taking a deeper look at the giants in your life and challenging them.

They may have good intentions, or they may have jealousy and poison-laden intentions; but we all have Eliabs in our lives who, if we listen to them, will keep us questioning and, by extension, from overcoming the challenges we encounter.

I had been a Christ-follower for about four years when I asked a prominent pastor a seemingly simple question: "Why is it that when I speak in churches or at Christian events around the country, they are always segregated?" God had tattooed a vision in my heart as a pastor. I believed there could be a church where black people, white people, Latino people, Asian people—people of all kinds, all ages, and all socioeconomic backgrounds—could come together, like the first-century church that transformed the Roman Empire. "I believe this can happen," I told him. "What do you think?"

He basically told me, "Well, that's a good dream, son, but you know the reality is that Sunday morning at church is the most segregated time in America. There's a reason for that. People of the same ethnic background and socioeconomic status are most comfortable together. It is a church's job, our job, to provide that comfortable environment for them. What you are trying to do will be very hard. Perhaps impossible." This pastor was an Eliab in my life.

Transformation Church was started on February 7, 2010, with 178 people. In just three years, God grew us into a multi-ethnic, multigenerational congregation of nearly twenty-two hundred, and more than fifteen hundred people had come to faith through the ministry of Transformation Church. In 2010, our first year in existence, we were the second-fastest-growing church in America by percentage. The next year, we were listed as one of the 100 fastest-growing churches in America, according to *Outreach* magazine.[4]

And to think, I almost let an Eliab keep me from planting Transformation Church.

Who are your Eliabs? What are they convincing you not to do for God? Don't let them limit the work Jesus wants to do in and through your life.

THE GOD WITHOUT LIMITS

From Fear to Faith

Planting Transformation Church has supercharged my life and caused me to grow spiritually at an exponential rate. I've learned to trust Jesus to accomplish incredible things. Often,

God will send us on a mission, and we won't know it because the mission is disguised as something else. I've lost track of the number of times I've gone to Starbucks to work on my sermon and ended up connecting with someone who needed to hear about Jesus' love as we talked over coffee. I've learned that He longs for His people to attempt the impossible so He can do the *Him*-possible.

As we were getting ready to start Transformation Church, we needed to turn an adjacent vacant lot, which closely resembled a jungle, into a parking lot. So we had a company give us an estimate of how much it would cost to construct one.

It would cost an estimated thirty thousand dollars, which was a lot more than the pocket lint and chewing gum in our bank account. And that was not even for a *paved* parking lot, but just a parking lot with rocks! Who knew rocks cost so much? So we did what we do best. We prayed. God longs for His people to pray prayers that make Him smile and say, "My children really do think I'm amazing." So we prayed a big, *courageous* prayer: "God, show us Your glory by providing the money for this parking lot."

The next week my wife, Vicki, had a dream that the owner of the company came to her and said, "God told us to do the parking lot for free." She didn't tell anyone but me.

Another week or so went by, and we saw the owner of the company at a flag football game. I coached his son. After the game he asked my wife, "Are you guys still wanting to do a parking lot?"

"Yeah," she answered, "but we don't have the money at this time."

He said, "God told us to do the parking lot for free."

Because of God's faithfulness in the past, I can be courageous in the future. And so can you.

The men of Israel would not fight Goliath because they had imposed their own limitations on God. They forgot that God is without limits. And because they forgot who God was, they limited who they could become. Sadly, we do the same.

Look at 1 Samuel 17:32–33: "And David said to Saul, 'Let no man's heart fail because of him. Your servant will go and fight with this Philistine.' And Saul said to David, 'You are not able to go against this Philistine to fight with him, for you are but a youth, and he has been a man of war from his youth.'"

Let's examine this conversation more closely.

"And David said to Saul . . ." This was a teenager speaking to an adult, and not just any adult, but the king. Now, that's courageous.

"Let no man's heart fail because of him." David didn't care how big Goliath was. He only knew how big his God was. The bigger we believe God to be, the bigger our courage will be, and the greater risk we will take to bring His name fame through our lives.

How about you? Do you look at the size of your giant, or do you look at the size of your God? The more we focus on the bigness of our God, the smaller our Goliaths become. The more we focus on the bigness of our Goliaths, the smaller our God becomes. Do you want to live a limitless life? If so, focus on how big, how loving, how powerful God is.

Young David said, "Your servant will go and fight with this Philistine." Notice the humility of this courageous young man of God: "Your servant." David's conversation wasn't peppered with "I . . . I . . . I." He saw himself as the king's humble servant. Throughout history, God has placed humble people in position to glorify His name—because they were willing to be servants.

"And Saul said to David"—here comes some discouragement—"'You are not able to go against this Philistine to fight *with him, for you are but a youth, and he has been a man of war from his youth.'"* The king of Israel, Saul, was telling David that Goliath was a champion, a king of sorts, "but you, you're just a little boy." Saul minimized, marginalized, and underestimated the limitless God that David knew and worshiped. Saul's own "Afraid" label had already limited him, so he was attempting to impose the same limitations on David.

Do you know some well-meaning people who project their fears onto you? "The economy is bad; you can't start a mortgage business. It will never work." That's what someone told my friends Casey and Michelle Crawford, who are Transformation Church members. At the height of the recession in 2008, God gave them a vision for a new kind of mortgage company. They wanted to honor Christ in how they conduct business, and they wanted a significant amount of the company's profits to go to making a difference in the lives of hurting and disadvantaged people. Instead of *talking* about change, Casey and Michelle want to *be* the change they long to see.

I remember when Casey shared their vision for the mortgage company with me while sitting at a coffee shop. He told me the odds were stacked against them, and it seemed impossible. I told him, "I believe in you. I believe in the God you want to honor with this vision. You can do it because of the One who will do it through you."

In just three years, Movement Mortgage has grown from ten employees to more than a thousand and is one of the fastest-growing mortgage companies in America. What God has accomplished through this courageous, faith-filled couple is limitless.

What have you been told God can't do through you? Don't let the fear-induced limitations of others limit you. We must be like David and refuse to allow fear to keep us from our destinies.

Key 4: Remember God's Past Faithfulness

David was courageous because he saw the bigness of God in his past. While David was protecting sheep, God had empowered him to slay lions and bears. This past experience with God prepared him for his future battle with Goliath.

Slow down for a moment and consider how God has been faithful to you in the past. Draw strength and courage from how He has kept His promises to you. God's past faithfulness gives us courage in the present and hope for the future.

What causes a teenage boy to fight a giant? What would motivate David to do something so ridiculous and impossible? When God sews the "Courageous" label in your heart, what seems ridiculous and impossible to most people makes sense and becomes possible.

David was motivated by God's glory and empowered by His strength. He had faith in God's past faithfulness to him. God wants His glory to inspire you. He created you to do something unique for His glory. He wants to be your strength as you fulfill that task.

When you live in fear, you limit the impact of what God desires to accomplish through you. You don't have time to live in fear. There is too much for you to accomplish. God has future accomplishments with your name written on them. Go get them.

Key 5: Wear God's Armor

Just as David was about to go fight Goliath, King Saul decided to dress David in his battle armor. I like the way Eugene Peterson describes this interaction in *The Message*:

"Then Saul outfitted David as a soldier in armor. He put his bronze helmet on his head and belted his sword on him over the armor. David tried to walk but he could hardly budge. David told Saul, 'I can't even move with all this stuff on me. I'm not used to this.' And he took it all off" (1 Sam. 17:38–39). David could not walk, let alone fight Goliath now with all that armor on. Why? Because it was someone else's armor. God had special armor, tailor-made for David, and it would be the same armor he had worn when he took care of the sheep: his staff, his slingshot, and rocks.

David sprinted toward the giant, shouting like a warrior whose heart was set on fire with God's courage, saying:

> You come to me with a sword and with a spear and with a javelin, but I come to you in the name of the LORD of hosts, the God of the armies of Israel, whom you have defied. This day the LORD will deliver you into my hand, and I will strike you down and cut off your head. And I will give the dead bodies of the host of the Philistines this day to the birds of the air and to the wild beasts of the earth, that all the earth may know that there is a God in Israel, and that all this assembly may know that the LORD saves not with sword and spear. For the battle is the LORD's, and he will give you into our hand. (1 Sam. 17:45–47)

As I read these words, tears fill my eyes, my heart pounds, and something deep within me yearns to live this kind of limitless life. That yearning we feel is God calling courage out of us to be displayed in this world that desperately needs courageous people. God won the battle through David. The battle was not even close. It was a rout of epic proportions.

MARINATE ON THAT!

First, God has a special, tailor-made armor suit that He lovingly and sacrificially made with His own hands for you too. Listen with your heart: "You were baptized into union with Christ, and now you are clothed, so to speak, with the life of Christ himself" (Gal. 3:27 GNT).

When you trusted Jesus as the One who died for your sins and as the One who rose again, you got the greatest gift of all—Him. Your worth is solidified by Jesus allowing Himself to be made a bloody mess on the cross. And it's true: you are not good enough—but Jesus is! And because He's good, He makes you good enough to be loved by His Father.

Second, don't wear anybody else's armor when going into battle against your Goliaths. What does that mean? It means life is too short to waste it trying to live somebody else's life. Take your staff, your slingshot, and grab your five rocks. Use the gifts and abilities God has given *you*, and sling them at the giants you will face.

Key 6: Know You Are Loved

As I peer back into my past, I believe that at the root of all "Afraid" labels and actions motivated by fear is the question, "Am I unconditionally loved?" In the depths of life's deepest pits, how we answer this question will stitch into our hearts either the "Afraid" label or the "Courageous" label.

So, what do you think? With God on our side like this, how can we lose? If God didn't hesitate to put everything on the line for us, embracing our condition and exposing himself to the worst by sending his own Son, is there anything else he wouldn't gladly and freely do for us? And who would dare tangle with God by messing with one of God's chosen? Who would dare even to point a finger? The One who died for us—who was raised to life for us!—is in the presence of God at this very moment sticking up for us. Do you think anyone is going to be able to drive a wedge between us and Christ's love for us? There is no way! Not trouble, not hard times, not hatred, not hunger, not homelessness, not bullying threats, not backstabbing, not even the worst sins listed in Scripture:

> They kill us in cold blood because they hate you.
> We're sitting ducks; they pick us off one by one.

None of this fazes us because Jesus loves us. I'm absolutely convinced that nothing—nothing living or dead, angelic or demonic, today or tomorrow, high or low, thinkable or unthinkable—absolutely nothing can get between us and God's love because of the way that Jesus our Master has embraced us. (Rom. 8:31–39 MSG)

It all comes down to the question, "God, do You love me with no strings attached?" What do you believe that answer to be? Your answer makes all the difference in removing "Afraid" from your heart and replacing it with "Courageous." When you ruthlessly believe God is with you and that He loves you unconditionally, you will face even the greatest of life's challenges with limitless courage because you know the God without limits is closer to you than your next breath.

JESUS DEFEATS ALL YOUR GIANTS

Before we move into our Transformation Moment at the end of this chapter, it is important to understand the historical-redemptive meaning of the David and Goliath story. Here's something we can't miss.

The story of David and Goliath is actually a picture of what Jesus came to do in history on behalf of humanity. David was a shepherd. Jesus is the Great Shepherd. Israel was afraid and weak. You and I are afraid and weak. David defeated Goliath. Jesus defeated Goliath. Who was the "Goliath" Jesus defeated? Jesus defeated sin, death, and Satan.

Jesus defeated the sin that causes us to alienate ourselves from God, from ourselves, and from one another. Then, when He died and rose from the dead, death was defeated too. Jesus said, "I am the resurrection and the life. Anyone who believes in me will live, even after dying. Everyone who lives in me and believes in me will never ever die" (John 11:25–26 NLT). When Jesus walked out of the tomb, death was not allowed to come out and make us afraid anymore.

The apostle Paul said, "Death is swallowed up in victory. O death, where is your victory? O death, where is your sting?" (1 Cor. 15:54–55).

Jesus also defeated Satan through His victory.

When you were spiritually dead because of your sins and you were not yet free from the power of your sinful self, God made you alive with Christ, and He forgave all our sins. He canceled the debt, which listed all the rules we've failed to follow. He took away that record with its rules and nailed it to the cross. God also stripped the spiritual rulers and powers of their authority. With the cross, He won the victory and showed the world that they were powerless. (Col. 2:13–15 NCV)

On the third day, Courage Himself walked out of that tomb. When Jesus came out, He made it possible to live His courageous, limitless life through His followers. The church is a community of courageous giant-slayers because of Him.

Go now. Slay those giants. Courage is who you are, because of who Jesus is.

TRANSFORMATION MOMENT

Head

Read 1 Samuel 17:45–47. In Christ—the One who defeated sin, death, and Satan (Goliath)—the Lord God is with you. He is your courage and He fights your battles.

Let this truth wallpaper your mind. And believe it.

Heart

Pray:

Father God, though fear surrounds me, I choose to hide and find my strength and courage in Your Son, Jesus. By the Spirit's power, Jesus is my courage, and in Him I am more than a conqueror. Today I refuse to let fear keep me from my destiny. I choose courage in Jesus! I'm available for You to do the inconceivable through me, for Your glory. In Jesus' name, amen.

Hands

- Make a list of all the things you are afraid of, write an *X* on them, and then burn the list. Then make a list of ways God has been faithful to you in the past. Put it somewhere you will see it often.
- Read Romans 8:35–39.

TWO

FROM ADDICT TO FREE

I WANT TO INTRODUCE YOU TO HERBERT. HERBERT IS A MEMBER OF Transformation Church, and he is my friend. But he wasn't always my friend, or a member of Transformation Church. Here's the story of how we met.

One evening my family and I went to dinner with friends at an Italian restaurant near our home in Charlotte, North Carolina. At the time, my daughter, Presley, was twelve, and my son, Jeremiah, was just seven. Presley is an adventurous eater, just like I am. Jeremiah will eat a wide variety of food too—as long as it is cheese and bread. So he was not happy when he found out we would be dining at an Italian restaurant. And like most kids his age, he let us know this by having a bad attitude. On the way to the restaurant, he was cranky. In the parking lot, he was cranky. And when we sat down at our table—you got it—he was cranky.

But then a big man with an even bigger smile arrived at our table to serve us. Immediately his booming yet cheerful voice captured our attention; even Jeremiah's pouting turned around. The hospitality this man exuded was beyond the typical "I'm going to be nice to you so you can give me a good tip."

As I looked into the eyes of the big man, I sensed his heart was even bigger than his smile. It still brings tears to my eyes, remembering how that big man with the big smile won my son's heart. But he didn't stop there. He charmed everyone at the table. We were under his spell.

Before I knew it, he had Jeremiah and Presley creating multiflavored drinks with him at the pop machine. Jeremiah was having so much fun he had forgotten he didn't want to be there. What a great night! The service was remarkable. The food was magnificent. But the night was about to get even better.

As we and our greatly expanded stomachs were getting ready to leave the restaurant, I sensed a prompting from God and said to the big man with the big smile, "Herbert, God has a call on your life. He has placed a massive amount of love in your heart. God has gifted you to make people happy. Get ready: God is going to do something in your life."

I do not believe in chance encounters. In every moment of every day that has ever been, God—Master Conductor of the symphony of life that He is—orchestrates every encounter we have with others. I believe that before time began, God envisioned the day I'd encounter Herbert. All my past experiences were for this moment. I believe this about every encounter with every person I have. Having this Christocentric perspective keeps me aware, present, and appreciative of people.

For the last fifteen years, I've made it a habit to carry my NFL trading cards with me. What's unique about them is that instead of having my football statistics on the back, I have the story of how I came to faith in Jesus. At restaurants, I leave a generous tip, my autographed trading card, and a church business card, in hopes that the server will connect with our church. Normally I don't put my personal phone number on the card, but this time I sensed I needed to.

About two weeks later, I got a phone call from the big man with the big smile. For the first few moments, our conversation was pretty light. Then Herbert's booming yet cheerful voice began to crack. That crack soon broke into deep sobbing.

Have you ever heard the agony in another person's cry and sensed the pain that is breaking his heart? Herbert said, "Pastor, I'm tired of living a lie. I'm an addict, and it's killing me and the people I love. My addiction has cost me my children, my family, and my money. It has stolen everything from me. I'm tired, Pastor. I'm tired. Can you help me?"

Herbert had an "Addict" label in his heart. The chains of addiction had limited him.

ADDICTS DON'T SUFFER ALONE

Addiction is a cruel master whose sole objective is to destroy the addict—and anyone else in his or her life. No addict ever suffers alone.

Here is Herbert's description of how addiction ruined his and his loved ones' lives:

Because of my addiction, I was lonely, mad, and always frustrated. I was always out in the streets, wanting to get my next drink or hit. It was devastating. I was a slave. I constantly worried about how others felt and thought about me. I tried to hide my addiction by cleaning myself up. No matter how hard I tried to hide it, my family knew. Addiction has separated me from my family for years. It cost me my first marriage. My children don't even know who I am. My darkest days of being an addict felt like I was snatching my family's life away from them. I was out one night, smoking crack, and I ran out. I knew I had to get more. I wanted more. I was craving more.

My sister wanted me to go grocery shopping for her. She gave me several hundred dollars to do it. It was tough because as I walked to her house, I was telling myself, "Don't do it. Don't do it. Don't do it." When she handed me the money, I knew I wasn't coming back. I knew my family was going to go without food. But it didn't matter because I wanted to get high.

Herbert's addiction touched many: wife, sister, children . . . who knows how many more? An addict never suffers alone.

ADDICTS DON'T HARM JUST THEMSELVES

Have you ever seen a town that has been flattened by a tornado? The devastation is almost beyond description. It looks like something from an apocalyptic science fiction movie.

Cars are flung like rag dolls. Homes are obliterated as if they are made of straw. And people's lives are shattered.

In some ways, addiction is like a tornado. The addict's life is flung around like a rag doll. His or her families and friends are battered and beaten emotionally, sucked dry financially, and many times physically beaten as well. Addiction is a black hole that sucks in everyone touched by it. The "Addict" label is ruthless. The plague of addiction has been especially cruel to my family, holding an entire generation at gunpoint and abducting their potential.

I came from a very talented family. I think of the comedians who could have lightened the world, the entrepreneurs who could have brought innovations to their communities. When I think of the greatness that has been lost to this cruel thief, it breaks my heart.

One of the reasons I'm so passionate about Jesus and His kingdom is that I want, by God's grace, to undo the pain and hurt that addiction has mercilessly unleashed on my family. So many hopes, so many dreams, so much potential that could have made a difference in this world have gone unrealized because of various addictions.

One of my much older cousins was a great basketball player. Perhaps I was not the only one from the family who should have been a professional athlete. But his career and life were limited by addiction. The last time I saw my cousin alive, I was preaching at my grandfather's funeral. He leaned forward and hung on every word I preached that day! I could hear him saying, "Look at little Dewey preach! That boy can preach!" As I preached, I wondered if he was remembering the days when he would take me with him to basketball games that he officiated when I was a little boy.

As I write this chapter, I'm thinking about his own funeral. I'm not sad, though, because the Great Liberator, named King Jesus, the One who breaks the chains of addiction, had transformed my cousin's life. The tears I cry right now are tears of joy! My cousin went from this life to the next with a new label, "Free." The "Addict" label no longer defined him.

I boldly proclaim in Jesus' name that there will be a day that addiction will finally be defeated in my family. And all the potential that could have been will be. My family will be limitless.

ADDICTS AREN'T JUST ONE TYPE

The face of addiction has changed in the twenty-first century. It is no longer just the bum hustling in the streets to get his next bottle of cheap wine. The "Addict" label manifests itself in so many different and unexpected forms.

Addiction is now found in the suburban, upper-middle-class soccer moms hooked on prescription drugs. It is consuming the college sophomore at a prestigious Ivy League university addicted to gambling. It is destroying the teenagers who have to smoke some weed to make it through their classes in high school. It is affecting the twenty-somethings' seemingly innocent consumption of technology in the form of online gaming and social media.

Every day in America more and more people wear the "Addict" label.

The Porn-Addicted Pastor

Years ago I was at a speaking engagement, and on one of the evenings I tackled the issue of pornography. As the grace of God, like rain falling on scorched ground, touched the hearts of those attending, many of them ran to the front of the stage. You could hear the brokenhearted weeping as they confessed their need for help. They saw that Jesus did not run toward them with a clenched fist but with open arms, to give them a divine embrace of grace. These precious people saw that Jesus did not hide from their sin, but ran toward the cross to die for them. It was a beautiful night.

After about two hours of counseling several of those who

came forward, I dragged myself to my room, around 1:30 a.m. As I was getting ready to fall into a coma-like sleep, I thanked Jesus for the opportunity to display His grace. John 1:16 marinated my mind: "For from his [Jesus'] fullness we have all received, grace upon grace."

Right as I was entering the "promised land" of sleep, there was knocking on my door. I must admit: Jesus-centered thoughts did not flood my mind. As I made my way from the bed to the door, I was contemplating how I was going to tell the individual on the other side that we'd have to talk over breakfast in the morning.

When I opened the door, I was stunned to see the shame-smeared face of a man of influence. He said, "Derwin, can I please come in? I need to talk with you."

God was very gracious to me. All my tiredness went away and was replaced with energy. I listened to this man torn apart by guilt, as he shared his struggle with a pornography addiction, until the early hours of the morning. The "Addict" label had so dominated his life that he was even risking discovery by watching porn in his office. He was a very effective communicator, and that compounded matters. He was so naturally gifted that he could speak against such sins while committing them. On the outside he looked great, but on the inside his addiction was like a cruel, aggressive form of cancer. His soul was being eaten away. Underneath the applause and accolades he received for speaking with power and effectiveness was a suffering addict on spiritual life support.

ADDICTS DON'T COMPREHEND THEIR WORTH

Humans have an amazing ability to get addicted to just about anything—food, shopping, people-pleasing, and self-pleasing.

The reason for our addictive appetites is that we were created for worship. Worship has a powerful impact on us in that we draw our identity, worth, and purpose from the object of our worship. *Identity* tells us who we are. *Worth* gives us our value. *Purpose* gives us a reason for waking up every morning.

While we were created for worship, it was not intended for the many external things we fixate on. God intended that He would be the target of our worship because He created humanity to draw our identity, worth, and purpose from being loved by Him. God says we are His beloved children and that we are valuable because Jesus died for us. God says we have a purpose—to know Him and make Him known through our lives. This is the essence of worship.

If we don't discover our identity, worth, and purpose in God through Jesus, we will find and worship a substitute god. Substitute gods promise freedom but only succeed in enslaving us. At the root of every addiction is idolatry—the futile effort of going to a substitute god to meet our needs. Instead of going to Jesus to meet our needs, we turn to shopping, sex, drugs, alcohol, food, or work to meet them.

As I talked with a woman who had a charismatic, warm, and loving personality, I thought, *What an incredibly gifted person*. Sadly, her drug and alcohol addiction, like a ruthless thief, had stolen her life and the potential that could have been.

When she was about nine, her grandfather had sexually abused her. This horrible act of evil shredded her soul. Immediately she embraced the message that she wasn't worth anything. Having come from a family that sweeps things under the rug, she felt she couldn't tell anyone. As the years went by, all she could do was replay over and over what happened to her. This multiplied her pain and refreshed her wounds. She told me, "Pastor, I just wanted the pain to end. Alcohol and drugs took the pain away, for a little while."

To numb the pain, she started getting high as a teenager and drinking cheap wine. This progressed to taking prescription pills, which escalated to shooting heroin and then to smoking crack. Instead of going to Jesus, who suffered for her on the cross and with her through her years of heartache, she went to substitute gods that only added to her hurt.

ADDICTS DON'T KNOW FREEDOM

For those who have never truly grappled with a severe addiction, the choice seems obvious. *Why wouldn't you simply choose freedom from this kind of pain and destruction?* Well, once you are in the grips of these addictions, once the label of "Addict" has been stitched on your heart, it is so much easier said than done.

One of my favorite movies is *Inception*, starring Leonardo DiCaprio. His character, Dom Cobb, leads a team of spies who are hired by corporations to steal valuable information from their rivals. Cobb and his team pull off some specialized espionage by entering into the dreams of executives through special military technology to extract top secret information.

The movie's plot leaps off the screen when a corporation hires Cobb and his crew to do an "inception"—the planting of an idea in the minds of targets from a rival corporation. Cobb had done this only one other time.

Watching this film, it occurred to me that this is what Satan and his demons do to humanity. They want to steal God's truth from our minds (extraction) and then implant lies about God and us in our minds (inception).

The movie's tagline is, "Your mind is the scene of the crime."

That is so true, and this is precisely what happens with addiction. If we don't know who we are and whose we are, we will not know how to live in the world. This leads us to seek false gods to meet our needs. The result is addiction.

MARINATE ON THAT!

The truth is, we do not have addiction problems. We have misdirected worship. I'm convinced every human being is in recovery and being weaned from some form of addiction because of idolatry. Your addiction or mine may not have us eating out of trash cans, but our sin habit is hurting and diminishing God's glory in our lives.

TIME FOR A NEW LABEL ... "FREE"

As we move into the practical steps of ripping the "Addict" label from our hearts and replacing it with the "Free" label, I want to wallpaper your mind with gospel truth about *who you are*. This gospel truth will encourage your heart regarding *whose you are*. Then we will look at taking steps to freedom so you'll know *how to live in this world*. Following are the keys for making the transformation from addict to free:

Key 1: Know Who You Are

The victory over sin and addiction has already been won. We just need to believe it. Because the scene of the crime is our minds, we have to fight for freedom from addiction *in our minds*.

Satan and his demonic forces do not want you to know who you are in Christ, because if you did, a revolt and rebellion against him would ensue. Let's feed on the apostle Paul's words:

> Have you forgotten that when we were joined with Christ Jesus in baptism, we joined him in his death? For we died and were buried with Christ by baptism. And just as Christ was raised from the dead by the glorious power of the Father, now we also may live new lives. Since we have been united with him in his death, we will also be raised to life as he was. We know that our old sinful selves were crucified with Christ so that sin might lose its power in our lives. We are no longer slaves to sin. For when we died with Christ we were set free from the power of sin. (Rom. 6:3–7 NLT)

Notice Paul asks us a question: "Have you forgotten . . . ?"

Demonic forces want to distract you from knowing the gospel truth about Jesus and yourself. You have been united to Jesus in His death and resurrection. This gospel truth is simply astonishing. When Jesus died on the cross, supernaturally you hung on the cross with Him. You were buried with Him in Joseph of Arimathea's tomb in Jerusalem. And on the third day, when Jesus rose from the dead, so did you. But now you are a new kind of you, with a new source of life. Jesus is now your life.

This transformation is so complete that when God the Father looks at you, He sees Jesus—not your past failures or even your accomplishments. He doesn't see the pain your sin or addiction has caused you and your loved ones. He sees Jesus in you. God's grace is just that amazing.

It seems too incredible to believe, doesn't it? This is why the gospel means "good news." Because of our union life with Jesus, we are no longer addicts. Instead, we are free. We just need to learn how to walk in the freedom that has already been won by Jesus.

Let's take a closer look at what this new identity means. Who are you in Jesus? You have become all the things you need to wear your new label, "Free."

Who Are You? Loved

Before Christopher Columbus ever arrived in America, God loved you. Before your daddy spotted your mom and thought she was hot, God loved you. Even in the midst of your addiction, He still loved you. Let Ephesians 1:4 drip into your soul: "Even before he made the world, God loved us and chose us in Christ to be holy and without fault in his eyes" (NLT).

Legendary country singer Willie Nelson was one of several artists who made the song "Always on My Mind" famous. Those are powerful words, but there is only One who can actually say them and be telling the truth. He is the Father, Son, and Holy Spirit! There has never been a moment that you were not on God's mind. There has never been a moment God has not loved you.

This eternal, redemptive love becomes real and better than life when you discover that Jesus has been pursuing you your whole life, even in the midst of addiction, hurt, and pain. He's always been there, saying, "I love you." When you look at the blood-soaked cross, know that He is saying to you now, "You were always on My mind."

The man I mentioned earlier who was addicted to porn did not understand God's love; neither did he allow Jesus to live through him. He was well versed in theology, but not God's love-ology. He found his identity and worth in speaking across America to large audiences. His platform was his substitute god, his drug of choice that temporarily met his emotional need for worth. When that no longer filled the hole in his heart, he turned to pornography. What was once a self-medicating mechanism was now a raging monster called addiction that no longer numbed his pain. It exacerbated it!

In those early-morning hours, I walked him through Ephesians 3:14–21:

> I bow my knees before the Father, . . . [asking] that according to the riches of his glory he may grant you to be strengthened with power through his Spirit in your inner being, so that Christ may dwell in your hearts through faith—that you, being rooted and grounded in love, may have strength to comprehend with all the saints what is the breadth and length and height and depth, and to know the love of Christ that surpasses knowledge, that you may be filled with all the fullness of God. Now to him who is able to do far more abundantly than all that we ask or think, according to the power at work within us, to him be glory in the church and in Christ Jesus throughout all generations, forever and ever. Amen.

I kept pushing into God's grace. He kept telling me how he was trying to stop his addiction, but the more he tried to stop, the worse it got. I told him, "You must stop trying to do what only Jesus can do; focus on God's love for you and how He wants to set you free by living through you." This went on for hours.

The next morning he approached me and said, "I get it. The God who loves me is the God who wants to live through me. I'm getting help."

Because of your union life with Jesus, God the Father loves you with the same intensity and passion that He loves

Jesus. You are what God the Father sees! You are not what you used to be! Who are you? Your name is *Loved*.

Who Are You? Holy and Faultless

Not only are you loved with a love that originated in eternity; through your union life with Jesus, you are also holy and faultless.

The word *holy* means "set apart for God's use." Holiness is not something obtained by spiritual Jedis who strive for it. Instead, it is given to spiritual beggars who, with empty hands, cling to Jesus and His cross. Holiness is a gift from God. Even before He made the world, God loved us and chose us in Christ to be holy and without fault in His eyes, "so now Jesus and the ones he makes holy have the same Father" (Heb. 2:11 NLT).

This gospel truth causes me to stagger because I'm drunk on God's love. When I look at my life and see how unholy I am, I'm amazed that God sees me as holy because I'm united with Jesus. Jesus' holiness is mine. And Jesus' holiness swallows us up.

You are also faultless. When God the Father looks at you, He doesn't see your faults, He sees His faultless Son (see Ephesians 1:5). You are holy *and* faultless, independent of your behavior. It's all dependent on Jesus' behavior, which God ascribes to you as a gift.

Who Are You? Forgiven

Not only are you loved, holy, and faultless; you are forever forgiven.

I want you to picture in your mind a courtroom. You are on trial for cosmic treason against God.

You are sitting on the right side, alone. The prosecuting attorney is seated on the left. In front is a Judge whose righteousness is so blinding you can't see His face; all you can see is His glory.

The well-dressed prosecuting attorney approaches the Judge. He turns on a twenty-foot, high-definition television. For hours he assaults you with everything you've ever done. His case is so convincing, so true, that it is beyond a shadow of a doubt that you are guilty of treason. You are guilty of being a sinner.

As you stand to receive your well-deserved sentence of eternity in hell from the Judge, the creaking sound of the door opening echoes through the courtroom. It's your defense attorney. He's wearing a ripped-up, blood-soaked robe. You notice He has holes in His wrists. As your attorney approaches the bench, a hush descends over the crowded courtroom, and under the silence you hear, "He's never lost a case."

The prosecuting attorney objects to your defense attorney representing you. He tells the Judge that he wants you to represent yourself.

The Judge speaks. The courtroom trembles at His voice as He says, "Shut your mouth. My beloved Son is about to speak!" And God's Son, your defense attorney, who was provided for you free of charge, says, "Daddy, everything the prosecution has said about My client is true. He is guilty. But I went to the cross and shed My blood to eternally secure My client's freedom and forgiveness."

God the Daddy, with a smile the size of the Milky Way, thunderously slams the gavel of heaven and joyfully shouts, "You, My child, are innocent of all charges against you. And you are forever forgiven!"

The woman I mentioned who was hurled into drug and alcohol addiction to numb the pain of her childhood sexual molestation has found freedom from her "Addict" label because Jesus' forgiveness has become real to her. She no longer looks at life through the rearview mirror of her past sins; she holds on to Jesus, who demonstrated her worth by dying for her. She's experienced freedom. The Great Proclamation of Emancipation has been signed in the blood of Jesus. The Great Liberator has replaced the "Addict" label with a new one: "Free."

Let Ephesians 1:7 soak in: "He is so rich in kindness and grace that he purchased our freedom with the blood of his Son and forgave our sins" (NLT). And God's forgiveness in Jesus is so complete that all your sins—past, present, and future—have been forgiven. The enemy of your soul loves to go historical on you. He reminds you of your sin or addiction. That's when you need to remind him of what Jesus accomplished on your behalf—you are *forever* forgiven.

Who Are You? God's Dwelling

Many people struggling with addiction have intense feelings of regret, shame, and guilt. The offspring of these toxic emotions is low self-esteem. If you ever want to know what a person thinks about herself, just watch what she does to herself. Many addicts feel worthless. (Remember, the scene of the crime is your mind.)

You are not worthless. You are so valuable that God the Daddy gave up the universe's most prized possession, Jesus, to purchase you. "God bought you with a high price," says 1 Corinthians 6:20 (NLT).

Do not move too fast over this gospel truth. *God bought you with a high price.* That high price was Jesus. He paid for you with the life of Jesus, to implant His life in you by the Spirit's power. Put on your spiritual seat belt, my friend, there's more:

Don't you realize that your body is the temple of the Holy Spirit, who lives in you and was given to you by

God? You do not belong to yourself, for God bought you with a high price. So you must honor God with your body. (1 Cor. 6:19–20 NLT)

In him you also are being built together into a dwelling place for God by the Spirit. (Eph. 2:22)

Who are you? *God's dwelling!* You are God's own temple!

In light of what Jesus has accomplished for us, we do not have the right to let our past tell our future what it is going to be. Your past sins have been killed. They are dead and buried. And Jesus officiated the funeral. So who are you now?

You are loved. You are holy and faultless. You are forgiven. And you are God's dwelling place. This is who you are.

If you are struggling with an addiction or deep-seated sin habit, it does not define you anymore. Jesus defines you. Hold on to this gospel truth. Because of your union life in Christ, you wear a new label—"Free"!

Key 2: Know Whose You Are

You belong to Jesus' Father and you belong to Jesus. God the Holy Spirit seals you forever to God the Father and God the Son. As a result of this gospel truth, you have a new nature, a new life force in you. That life force is Jesus Himself. You were born spiritually dead. But in Jesus you are now spiritually alive. The apostle says it this way: "Consider yourselves to be dead to the power of sin and alive to God through Christ Jesus" (Rom. 6:11 NLT).

The same Jesus who walked the dusty roads of Palestine is walking in you. The same Jesus who made a blind man see is living in you. The same Jesus who defeated Satan has made your heart His home. You are *without limits* because of the unlimited God who lives in you. Bite down on this gospel truth and do not let go.

Key 3: Know How to Live

Have you ever seen a lion try to fly like an American bald eagle? Have you ever seen a hamster try to put on a suit and work in corporate America? Have you ever seen a caterpillar try to speak in Spanish?

The answer to every one of these ridiculous questions is no! Why? Because the nature of each creation determines what it does in the world. Lions don't fly, hamsters aren't capable of taking on human traits, and caterpillars don't speak . . . in any language. But while it may seem a little absurd to suggest the stuff of fairy tales, we do much the same thing in our own lives without realizing it. So often we fail to understand our true nature and instead try to force ourselves into something unnatural. But when you know your true nature, you truly know how to live in the world.

According to Ephesians 2:3, before Christ our nature was "sinful" (NLT). This same verse goes on to say that we "were by nature children of wrath" (ESV). But in Christ, you and I share in the very nature of God Himself:

> By his divine power, God has given us everything we need for living a godly life. We have received all of this by coming to know him, the one who called us to himself by means of his marvelous glory and excellence. And because of his glory and excellence, he has given us great and precious promises. These are the promises that enable you to *share* his divine nature and escape the world's corruption caused by human desires. (2 Peter 1:3–4 NLT, emphasis added)

You have a new nature that is addiction resistant. In Christ, you are free. Soak for a moment in Romans 6:12–14, which says it this way:

> Do not let sin control the way you live; do not give in to sinful desires. Do not let any part of your body become an instrument of evil to serve sin. Instead, give yourselves completely to God, for you were dead, but now you have new life. So use your whole body as an instrument to do what is right for the glory of God. Sin is no longer your master, for you no longer live under the requirements of the law. Instead, you live under the freedom of God's grace. (NLT)

Because you know *who* you are—loved, holy, faultless, forgiven, and God's own dwelling place—you know *whose* you are! You belong to God the Father and His Son, Jesus. God the Holy Spirit seals you in this relationship eternally. Therefore, you now also know *how to live* in the world: "Give yoursel[f] completely to God, for you were dead, but now you have new life. So use your whole body as an instrument to do what is right for the glory of God" (v. 13 NLT).

In Christ, you have everything you need to beat any form of sin or addiction.

THE GOD WITHOUT LIMITS

What Was Intended for Evil, God Used for Good

When God has a destiny in mind for you, He will not allow the labels stitched in your heart or the hearts of those around you to limit what He can do through you. Take me: I should not be writing this book. I should be dead. That may sound melodramatic, but it's true. Here's what happened:

My family is late for everything. Even for funerals! I think I was about four, and my family was late getting to my great-grandfather's funeral. Several of my relatives and I piled into my grandfather's green Oldsmobile. One of my relatives was driving.

The driver, whom I loved immensely, was an addict. That day, behind the wheel, he was higher than a kite. His senses were dulled, his reactions were slowed, and his judgment was as cloudy as a thunderstorm.

As we approached a curve, going way too fast, his drug-induced mind could not react fast enough to slow down the car. Our car hit the guardrail, flew into the air, miraculously stopped in midair, and landed safely back on the road.

Once we gathered our composure, we jumped out of the car. I think I was in shock. My older cousin literally jumped into my mom's arms. I began to cry.

The relative who was driving jumped out of the car and broke down in tears. He sobbed, realizing an epic tragedy should have occurred that day, all because of his addiction.

One of the policemen who arrived on the scene said, "There is no way you all should be alive. This car should have rolled and rolled down this hill. You all should be dead."

My family member's addiction should have killed us.

Instead of just grieving one death that day, my family could have been grieving five more. On this occasion we were confronted with our mortality, the dangers of addiction, and how far-reaching those effects can be. But in most cases we will never know how close we come to death or how many times God intervenes on our behalf. Whether through the poor choices of others or attacks from the enemy, God's plan will not be limited by our destructive labels.

Perhaps God spared us that day so I could write this book just for you.

BREAKING FREE WITH JESUS

So what happened to Herbert, the big man with the big smile? I have great news to report. Herbert married a beautiful woman named Karen at Transformation Church, and I got to perform the ceremony. He now serves in our children's ministry and on the hospitality and worship teams. He also holds down a steady job helping homeless men.

Herbert has broken free from the "Addict" label. He's had some ups and downs. But he's doing great. When I see him onstage singing about Jesus' grace and tears flood his eyes, I'm looking at a man who has been set free.

Here are some steps we need to take if we want to walk in our new nature and continue the freedom we have received in Christ:

- *Confess* your sins. We must be honest with Jesus about our sin or addiction. Grace can only be poured into a broken heart. Confessing to Jesus is basically saying, "I am sick and tired of this sin [or addiction] destroying my life. Jesus, I need You."
- Live in *community*. We need each other. Each of us needs a community of people to walk alongside us— family members and friends whose primary job is to remind us of who we are and whose we are. They act

as a community of encouragers who keep Jesus and His grace always before you. Your community starts with your family, then your small group at your local church. Being reminded of who and whose you are will empower you to be who Jesus has already declared you to be.

- Get *counseling*. Counseling is very important. Some soul-wounds need professional attention. At Transformation Church we are developing a lay counseling team, and we also refer people to professional counselors. Many churches and community organizations have resources to help. Be humble and ask for the help you need.
- Have *courage*. Leaving the familiar surroundings of addiction is scary. Most people who are gripped by addiction try to hide from the real world. It takes courage to walk into the unknown, but we do not walk alone. Jesus walks before us, beside us, and in us.

Addiction will no longer limit you. You are without limits in Christ.

TRANSFORMATION MOMENT

Head

Remember this: in Christ, you are eternally loved, holy and faultless, forgiven, and God's dwelling place (Eph. 1:3–7; 2:22; 1 Cor. 6:19–20).

Heart

Pray:

Father, give me the courage to see what You see when You look at me. Lord Jesus, open my eyes and empower me to see what You see when You look at me. Holy Spirit, help me believe I am what You see when You look at me. I am loved! I am holy and faultless! I am forgiven! I am God's dwelling place! Therefore, I will be free from addiction. In Jesus' name, amen.

Hands

- We are all in recovery. Confess your sin issue or addiction to Jesus and to your community of encouragers.
- Go to counseling if you need to, and let Jesus be your courage.

THREE

FROM MESS TO MASTERPIECE

What an amazingly loving and sovereign God we have! He turns our messy life into a masterpiece work of art as we let Him do the work in and around us.

—Adrian Pantonial

THERE ARE TIMES IN OUR LIVES WHEN WE HAVE AN ENCOUNTER WITH someone and then say to ourselves, "There has to be a God." My friend Chien is one of those people. His life was a mess. I want to share the events of his life because he is a perfect example of how someone who seems to be a hopeless mess can be transformed into a masterpiece by God.

Chien's story:

I was born and raised in Vietnam. My sister and I, along with my aunt and cousins, were taken care of by my sixty-five-year-old grandmother. I do not know who my father is. He abandoned me before I was born. My mom left for the U.S. when I was three years old. There was no way a sixty-five-year-old lady could feed four other people and survive in the little village where we lived. So, in seventh grade I dropped out of school and ran away because I did not want to be a burden to my grandmother. When I look back at my life, I was a mess.

One of my neighbors had some land where he farmed watermelons, potatoes, and sugarcane. I made a deal with him. I went to work for him and stayed on his farm. I disappeared for three weeks, and I told him not to tell my grandmother where I was. After three weeks, I went back to our village and gave her some money. She wanted me to go to school, but I asked her to please let me help her provide for our family. I told her that if she did not let me, then I'd run away again. She agreed.

I continued to work for my neighbor. I built a straw hut on his land. This became my home. I'd drink water out of a creek. In 1979, we just about starved to death. We would go into the jungle, and whatever looked like it could be eaten, we ate! A couple of times we got food poisoning, and I thought we were going to die. It did not matter, though, because we were so hungry.

I never really got into a lot of crazy things, such as doing drugs or becoming an alcoholic. But I think there's something that is worse, that is more harmful than those things—the anger, the bitterness, and the resentment that was in my heart. My bitterness caused me not to trust people. I kept people at a distance and wouldn't open up because I was afraid of being hurt. I wasn't a very friendly person. I was angry and selfish. Everything I did was for me because growing up I had to fight for one scoop of rice.

*Not having my parents and growing up the way I did made me very angry, bitter, and resentful. As a little boy, I would dream that if I could just get to America, I would die a happy person.**

THE MESS OF TOXIC FEELINGS

Chien was angry, bitter, and resentful. He was a toxic mess, and who can blame him, considering his hellish circumstances?

The circumstances of life are never neat and tidy, and sometimes they cause us to become a mess ourselves. The three-headed monster called anger, bitterness, and resentment made Chien's heart toxic—a form of spiritual cancer. Toxic people are guarded and unfriendly because they are living out of their woundedness. Like an oil spill, their toxic and cancerous emotions spread and saturate those in their sphere of influence. These are individuals in need of spiritual chemotherapy. The spiritual chemotherapy we need is called the gospel of grace, and our spiritual oncologist is named Jesus. Jesus is full of grace, the kind of love and healing power that can neutralize the corrosive nature of toxic emotions. Through His grace, our tragedies will become triumphs. The biblical character Joseph's did. He told his jealous brothers, "You plotted evil against me, but God turned it into good, in order to preserve the lives of many people who are alive today because of what happened" (Gen. 50:20 GNT).

Consider Satan. He was once a beautiful and powerful archangel. He felt entitled to that position, but pride was his downfall. He wanted to take God's place as king of the

---

* Chien gave his testimony on September 15, 2011, at Transformation Church.

universe. Somehow Satan convinced other angels to join him in his rebellion against God. Satan and his minions were defeated. Their tragic strategic error did not work out for them, and God kicked them out of heaven.

Cast out, Satan nurtured a hatred for God that burned deep in his diseased heart and spilled over to humanity because we remind him of God. Like God, we are able to love, create, choose, and feel. Like Him, we each have a mind, will, and emotions. This is what it means to be made in God's image and likeness. Satan can't touch God, but he can touch and make a mess out of our lives. He started with Adam and Eve and plunged all their offspring into a messy world.

THE MESS WE MAKE

So, here's the big question: Why is life such a mess anyway?

Satan's desire to get revenge is a good place to start, but that is not the only place to lay blame. Being the lover that God is, He provided for Adam and Eve's every need in the garden. The only stipulation God had for them was to not eat from the Tree of the Knowledge of Good and Evil, because if they did, they would sever their connectivity to the very Source of life. They would die spiritually, and physical death would await them and their offspring. But not only would they die; even creation would become a mess.

One day Eve was admiring the fruit that hung from the Tree of the Knowledge of Good and Evil. As she admired it, Satan, who is the father of lies, deceived Eve into doubting God's goodness. Let's eavesdrop on their conversation:

The serpent was the shrewdest of all the wild animals the LORD God had made. One day he asked the woman, "Did

God really say you must not eat the fruit from any of the trees in the garden?"

"Of course we may eat fruit from the trees in the garden," the woman replied. "It's only the fruit from the tree in the middle of the garden that we are not allowed to eat. God said, 'You must not eat it or even touch it; if you do, you will die.'"

"You won't die!" the serpent replied to the woman. "God knows that your eyes will be opened as soon as you eat it, and you will be like God, knowing both good and evil."

The woman was convinced. She saw that the tree was beautiful and its fruit looked delicious, and she wanted the wisdom it would give her. So she took some of the fruit and ate it. Then she gave some to her husband, who was with her, and he ate it, too. (Gen. 3:1–6 NLT)

According to the Jesus Story, this is when the messiness of sin and death entered humanity. And we've been a mess ever since. But the mess that Adam and Eve caused is not just limited to humanity; it even negatively affects creation itself: "For we know that the whole creation has been groaning together in the pains of childbirth until now" (Rom. 8:22).

Just as my wife, Vicki, labored in the pain of childbirth to bring Presley and Jeremiah into this world, creation itself suffers labor pains, such as when a hurricane devastates or a tornado destroys. Creation awaits the day when this mess of a world will be healed.

As I ponder Chien's story, my heart breaks thinking about what he's gone through. I have a twelve-year-old son, and to think of him searching for food in a jungle hurts to just consider. Right now children around the world are experiencing the same pain Chien experienced.

Of course, it is normal for us to look at these situations and others like them and ask why it has to be this way. When we ask God this question, I believe it purges our souls. God is not afraid of our questions. Often, we are afraid of His answers, though. But His answers to our questions are always for our good, even when we do not understand. He loves taking messes and transforming them into masterpieces.

KEYS TO BECOMING A MASTERPIECE

Key 1: Understand We Live in a Messy World

Every person has a way of seeing life—his or her world-view—through which the individual interprets what happens in life. For the follower of Christ, the Jesus Story is our navigational framework by which we interpret life, similar to a spiritual GPS. According to the Bible, where the Jesus Story is found, humanity was born into a messy world because of Adam and Eve, humanity's first parents: "You know the story of how Adam landed us in the dilemma we're in—first sin, then death, and no one exempt from either sin or death. That sin disturbed relations with God in everything and everyone" (Rom. 5:12–13 MSG). The world was a mess . . . but it wasn't always that way.

His-Story, His Mission

As God created, His genius was on full display. At the end of the first five days of His work, He said, "This is good." (You can read this story in Genesis 1.)

But on the sixth day of creation, God unveiled His masterpiece. This work of art, which made all creation stand in awe, was His image bearer. God admired His masterpiece and said it was "very good."

The image bearer, Adam, was the first human, according

to the Jesus Story. God created another image bearer, Eve, to be Adam's companion. Adam and Eve lived in a beautiful garden called Eden, which means "delight." God gave these first humans a mission. In essence He said, "I want you to rule and reign on earth the way I do in My dimension called heaven. I want you to enjoy each other and have a bunch of babies and fill this planet with more image bearers. Through you and your offspring, My mission to turn earth into a version of heaven will be fulfilled." Jesus echoed this truth when He taught His disciples how to pray, saying, "Thy kingdom come, Thy will be done in earth, as it is in heaven" (Matt. 6:10 KJV).

At first the image bearers thought God's plan was good, but then Lucifer, or Satan, devised a plan to destroy God's children and His dream, creating a mess in His creation.

God's Master Plan

God is the only Being in the universe who can never be surprised. God sees all history in one eternal glance. The past, present, and future are one simultaneous moment to God. He was not surprised at the fall of humanity. In the same way, He was not caught off guard when Chien was born in Vietnam. He wanted him there.

He was not surprised that I would be born on April 9, 1971, in San Antonio, Texas, to two teenagers. He wanted me there.

The fact that God determined where and when we'd be born doesn't mean we are preprogrammed robots. It means God supernaturally fulfills His purposes through humanity's messy, self-determined actions.

Key 2: Know That God Is Never Far from Us

When my friend Chien was running around in a Vietnamese jungle, starving, where was God?

That's a legitimate question. And God has a legitimate answer. Let's spend a moment walking through Acts 17:26–27: "From one man he created all the nations throughout the whole earth. He decided beforehand when they should rise and fall, and he determined their boundaries. His purpose was for the nations to seek after God and perhaps feel their way toward him and find him—though he is not far from any one of us" (NLT).

First, we learn from this text that God created humanity from Adam and Eve. There is only one race, the human race. Second, we learn that before time ever began, God knew when and where every human would live and die.

But why does God govern His universe this way? Verse 27 says that His purpose was for the nations—which means people of different ethnicities—to "seek God, and perhaps feel their way toward him and find him. Yet he is actually not far from each one of us." *God governs as He does so that people, no matter where they are, will search for Him, because He's really closer than we think.*

God was not far from Chien when his father and mother left him. He was not far away when Chien roamed the jungles, looking for food. And God was closer than Chien realized as he slept in a straw hut.

According to the Jesus Story, God was there and was using Chien's messy circumstances to draw Chien to Himself. Every ounce of fear, pain, and brokenness Chien experienced, Jesus experienced too—on the cross. All pain, all hopelessness, and all suffering for all time for every person was absorbed into Jesus at Calvary. No wonder Jesus said, "My Father, if it be possible, let this cup pass from me; nevertheless, not as I will, but as you will" (Matt. 26:39).

So, where is God in the midst of this messy world that

messes up our lives? He is orchestrating His universe with wisdom and care, not from a remote planet, but right next to us, suffering as we suffer. He is bringing about His purposes through the decisions we make and through every circumstance. And by grace, through faith in Jesus, we win in the end too.

The late Steve Jobs, founder of Apple Inc., once said, "You can't connect the dots looking forward; you can only connect them looking backwards."[1] When we're in a mess, we can't see any good in it, let alone a positive outcome. But when we enter in the Jesus Story, His grace turns our messes into masterpieces, defeats into victories, and pain into eternal pleasure.

Key 3: Throw a Party in the Pit

Can you imagine being ruthlessly beaten up, thrown into a pit, and sold as a slave in a foreign country, where you would be falsely accused of attempted rape and banished to die in prison? And to make matters worse, it was your older brothers who committed this unspeakable act of evil against you?

Well, that's exactly what happened to Joseph. Let's go behind the scenes and see how God was preparing to accomplish epic acts of greatness through Joseph, how He was planning to use a slave's messy circumstances to transform him into a masterpiece! God had a great call on Joseph's life, but before Joseph could ascend to the second-highest position in Egypt, he had to descend into a pit: "[Joseph's brothers] saw him from afar, and before he came near to them they conspired against him to kill him. . . . When Joseph came to his brothers, they stripped him of his robe, the robe of many colors that he wore. And they took him and threw him into a pit. The pit was empty; there was no water in it" (Gen. 37:18, 23–24).

God uses these low places to get us to surrender to

Him. He transforms us in these depths when we are rendered powerless. In the pit, Joseph learned humility. He also
learned how to love and forgive. That may not seem like a
difficult lesson, but it was an enormous obstacle, for it was
his own brothers who had thrown him into the pit and sold
him as a slave.

Then they sat down to eat. And looking up they saw
a caravan of Ishmaelites coming from Gilead, with their
camels bearing gum, balm, and myrrh, on their way to
carry it down to Egypt. Then Judah said to his brothers,
"What profit is it if we kill our brother and conceal his
blood? Come, let us sell him to the Ishmaelites, and let
not our hand be upon him, for he is our brother, our own
flesh." And his brothers listened to him. Then Midianite
traders passed by. And they drew Joseph up and lifted
him out of the pit, and sold him to the Ishmaelites for
twenty shekels of silver. They took Joseph to Egypt. . . .
Potiphar, an officer of Pharaoh, the captain of the guard,
an Egyptian, . . . bought him from the Ishmaelites who
had brought him down there. . . .

One day, when [Joseph] went into the house to do his
work and none of the men of the house was there in the
house, [Potiphar's wife] caught him by his garment, saying, "Lie with me." But he left his garment in her hand
and fled and got out of the house. . . . Then she laid up his
garment by her until his master came home, and she told
him . . . , "The Hebrew servant, whom you have brought
among us, came in to me to laugh at me. But as soon as I
lifted up my voice and cried, he left his garment beside me
and fled out of the house."

As soon as his master heard the words that his wife

spoke to him, . . . his anger was kindled. And Joseph's master took him and put him into the prison, the place where the king's prisoners were confined. (Gen. 37:24–28; 39:1, 11–20)

In prison, Joseph learned wisdom and patience. He was falsely accused, and the deck appeared to be stacked against him. But God's guidance and gifts in this darkness helped Joseph strategize a way out of prison: "But the Lord was with Joseph and showed him steadfast love and gave him favor in the sight of the keeper of the prison. And the keeper of the prison put Joseph in charge of all the prisoners who were in the prison. Whatever was done there, he was the one who did it. . . . And whatever he did, the Lord made it succeed" (Gen. 39:21–23).

It was in the pit that God was preparing Joseph for the future He had planned. He was molding Joseph to take his place in the palace as a great and godly leader—one who would be humble, loving, forgiving, patient, and wise. You can read the rest of Joseph's incredible story in Genesis 40–50.

Friend, you may be in a pit right now, but don't despise the pit, because God is doing some behind-the-scenes work. Throw a party in the pit, because God is preparing to unleash His limitless life in and through you!

MARINATE ON THAT!

I love when my wife wears pearls. Pearls are beautiful, and they magnify her beauty as they reflect off her gorgeous eyes. But did you know that a pearl is also a masterpiece created out of a mess?

A pearl is made when a foreign object is caught inside an oyster. This object irritates the oyster, often creating a wound, and in response, the oyster's defense mechanism launches. The oyster releases a substance called *nacre*, which coats the intruding foreign material. As thousands of layers of nacre coat the irritant, a beautiful pearl is formed. This process takes seven to eight years, which is the full life span of an oyster.

Irritating, injury-causing foreign matter is transformed into a masterpiece called a pearl, all because an oyster gets wounded. Because you and I are born into a fallen world, we, like the oyster, will get wounded. But God, in His grace, will turn us into a masterpiece as a result.

Key 4: Turn Tragedies into Triumphs

Let me take you back to a life-altering moment. My heart raced with anticipation. Despite the seventy thousand screaming fans in the stands, all I could hear was a deafening silence. My focus was sharp, like the edge of a razor blade.

It was game time. I was back in Texas, my home state, in the famous old Texas Stadium, getting ready to play against the Dallas Cowboys as a member of the Carolina Panthers. Several of my relatives were among the thousands who filled the stadium. Many more were watching on TV. What was supposed to be a homecoming for me ended up being the end of my football career.

I was running down on kickoff coverage, as I had done countless times, when I engaged a blocker. In the midst of making contact with him, my left foot got stuck in the turf. In the longest second of my life, I heard and felt ligaments snapping like rubber bands in my left knee. I also heard bone breaking. I'll never forget that grinding sound. I found myself lying in the middle of the field in excruciating pain. In that moment, I knew my career was over. I'd overcome several injuries as a football player, but this one was the knockout punch.

I was so angry with God! "What are You *doing*?" I exploded at Him. "I have a dream to play ten years in the NFL! God, this is my career! This is how I feed my family! What are You doing? I'm so angry right now! I'm not going to pray for a day."

I had been a Jesus-follower for a little over a year at that time, so like most immature, selfish children, I was having a temper tantrum. I was in the pit—and throwing a pity party.

My blown-out knee ended my season. The Panthers placed me on the injured reserve list. That meant I was still on the team, but I couldn't play for the rest of the season.

So guess what I did with all the spare time I now had on my hands. I did rehab on my knee for an hour each day; then I spent several more hours a day reading the Bible. While sitting in the cold tub, I learned to pray and be with God. And the more I read the Bible and prayed, the more God renovated my life. I became a better husband. I became a better father. And I became a better man.

Then something really strange started to happen. I began to see myself preaching in front of thousands of people and sharing with them what I was learning about Jesus. Up until that point in my life, I had never wanted to be a preacher. Now all I could think about was sharing the hope that is found in Jesus.

I was a sponge. Everything I read I shared with anyone who would listen. I simply could not contain the good news that was transforming me. Older and wiser Jesus-followers began to tell me, "Derwin, you are an evangelist." I'd say, "An evanga-what?"

I don't think God caused me to blow out my knee, but He did allow it to happen. And it was for my own good and

His glory. My injury has taught me three gospel truths that anchor my soul in the storms of life.

1. *Suffering accelerates spiritual maturity.* The New Testament author James said it this way: "Dear brothers and sisters, when troubles come your way, consider it an opportunity for great joy. For you know that when your faith is tested, your endurance has a chance to grow. So let it grow, for when your endurance is fully developed, you will be perfect and complete, needing nothing" (James 1:2–4 NLT).

   Our life challenges test us, and either we wallow in self-pity or we allow them to widen our perspective.

2. *Our disappointments are appointments.* Paul the apostle explained:

   > That's why we can be so sure that every detail in our lives of love for God is worked into something good. God knew what he was doing from the very beginning. He decided from the outset to shape the lives of those who love him along the same lines as the life of his Son. The Son stands first in the line of humanity he restored. We see the original and intended shape of our lives there in him. (Rom. 8:28–29 MSG)

   What we see as unfair, as God letting us down, as a devastating detour, God sees as a path of correction, as the necessary steps to getting us where He needs us to be.

3. *God is more concerned with character than comfort.* Christ sets the right example, as found in Philippians 2:5–8: "You must have the same attitude that Christ Jesus had. Though he was God, he did not think of equality with God as something to cling to. Instead, he gave up his divine privileges; he took the humble position of a slave and was born as a human being. When he appeared in human form, he humbled himself in obedience to God and died a criminal's death on a cross" (NLT).

God often moves us out of our comfort zones so He can shape us into the people He intends us to be.

What I had to learn is that while I was physically hurt, Jesus was healing my hurt soul. While my football career was ending, God was beginning my new pastoral career. I thought the end of my football career was a tragedy, but God saw a future triumph. He had better plans.

Thank You, Jesus.

THE GOD WITHOUT LIMITS

A Medical Masterpiece

I love my wife. More than any person on earth, she has loved me with a love that has brought the best out of me. Vicki and I have been together since we met my freshman year in college, and we just celebrated our twenty-first wedding anniversary.

Vicki is my hero. She's taught me so much about life. She came to faith before I did. I could not understand what was happening to her, but I liked it. Her transformation intrigued me. She could not put it into words, but she knew she wanted it to happen to me too.

Then on May 17, 2004, I thought I was going to lose my hero. On that life-defining day, my wife was diagnosed with thyroid cancer. As we walked out of the doctor's office, we could not find words for our devastation. All I could say was, "Oh no, not my baby!"

I was terrified. Vicki was too. What would we tell our kids, who were seven and three at the time?

On the first night we got the bad news, neither one of us could sleep. Every second seemed like an hour. We started crying. Then my wife, like the hero she is, began to quote Scripture. I quoted one back. This back-and-forth turned into a game of spiritual tennis, where we would serve each other hope with each promise of God that we quoted. Soon our tears of fear became tears of joy.

We can rejoice when we run into problems and trials, for we know that they help us cultivate the endurance that develops strength of character and our confident hope of salvation. This hope will not lead to disappointment. We know how dearly God loves us, because He has given us the Holy Spirit to fill our hearts with His love.

Going through cancer taught my wife and me three gospel truths that flow from Romans 5:3–5:

1. *Suffering produces endurance.* As fear marched around our minds like an invading army, we retreated deeper into Jesus. He became our fortress of hope. As we pressed into Him, Jesus grew our roots deeper and deeper into the soil of His great love. This made us stronger. It made us tougher.

2. *Endurance produces character.* I never, ever want to go through cancer again. But as we journeyed through the valley of death, our attention to Jesus and to life was heightened. We saw the world differently: colors were brighter, food was better, people became more valuable, and our passion for reaching people with the gospel intensified. As we pressed into Jesus, His character became our character. What became important to Him became important to us. Our capacity to love and not sweat the small stuff increased exponentially.

3. *Character produces hope because we know we are loved by God.* My wife is cancer-free. I praise God. But even if she had died, I would still praise God, because our hope in the resurrection became a reality for us during our struggle. As death knocked on our door, we opened it and said, "Jesus is the resurrection and life. Though we die, we shall live." (See John 11:25.)

As a pastor I have preached at many funerals about the hope found in Jesus, but now it is personal. The resurrection of Jesus meant that if my wife had died, I would see her again at the resurrection. Because of His resurrection, even creation itself will be redeemed and made new (Rev. 21:1–4).

As we look back at our cancer scare, we both now see that God used the messiness of disease to make us faith-filled, strong, and tough enough to plant Transformation Church.

After you have experienced cancer, trusting God to provide a building to plant a church is small potatoes.

I imagine many of you reading my book are going through some messy, soul-wrenching circumstances. Please know that God is behind the scenes, using your mess to transform you into a masterpiece.

THE MASTERPIECE OF JESUS IN US

I [Chien] remember I used to dream, if I can live in the U.S. for just one day, I would die a very happy person. I didn't know then that God was going to bless me with more than one day. When I was a teenager, my mother reached out to me and invited me to come live with her in America.

When I came to the U.S., my stepfather and my mom asked me if I wanted to know about Jesus. At this time, I had already been in the U.S. for about a year, and they had been encouraging me to read the Bible. I started reading the Gospel of John. On the night of June 23, 1998, at 10 o'clock at night in our house, in Calistoga, California, I said, "Sure, let's talk." So we sat down and talked; they explained to me what it meant to be saved. Everything that I had learned about Buddhism, which is my family's religion, went out the window. I felt at that moment that Jesus cared about me. I gave my heart to Him that night.

Since we've been at Transformation Church, I've changed. My family has changed too. My wife shared with me that since we've been at Transformation Church, her heart is becoming more tender. Our small group's members are the most genuine people you could ever be around. I'm so glad that we get to be a part of this

> *community. Even though I was a mess and came from terrible circumstances, God has made my heart merciful and tender. There is nothing more important than God working in your heart and transforming you day by day.**

People like Chien are the reason we planted Transformation Church! Chien serves on our worship team. He is an amazing musician. As he plays his guitar, you feel the deep work God has done in his life. He and his wife also serve in our children's ministry. Career-wise, Chien is a general manager of a very successful car dealership. The same boy who was abandoned by his parents, who grew up foraging for food in the jungles of Vietnam, now has an amazing family and a thriving career.

God took Chien's "Mess" label and replaced it with "Masterpiece." He can do the same for you.

*For we are God's masterpiece. He has created
us anew in Christ Jesus, so we can do the
good things he planned for us long ago.*

Ephesians 2:10 NLT

---

* Chien gave his testimony September 15, 2011, at Transformation Church.

TRANSFORMATION MOMENT

Head

According to the Jesus Story, from which we interpret life, we are born into a messy world that has the potential to limit the life God desires for us. But God in His grace sent Jesus into our mess to transform us into masterpieces. Remember: suffering accelerates spiritual maturity, our disappointments are appointments, and God is more concerned with character than comfort.

Heart

Pray:

Lord Jesus, thank You. You not only understand my suffering, but You are intimately acquainted with every ounce of fear, pain, and brokenness every human has ever experienced. The weight of our mess fell on You when You suffered and died on the cross. No wonder You said, "My Father, if it be possible, let this cup pass from me" [Matt. 26:39]. Lord, not only do You understand my mess, but You were made a bloody, disfigured mess on the cross so that by Your grace I can be transformed into a masterpiece. Lord, I choose to now see adversity as an opportunity to know You more and make You known. Amen.

Hands

- Focus on Ephesians 2:10: "For we are God's masterpiece. He has created us anew in Christ Jesus, so we can do the good things he planned for us long ago" (NLT). Then take a moment and think about the ways God has used the messes of your life to prepare you to do something for His glory.

FOUR

FROM ORPHAN TO ADOPTED

We roam through life lost, looking for a love and identity that no human, no job, no amount of money could ever provide. Our Papa in heaven is the only One who can provide us with the love and, ultimately, the identity we have been created for—a child of God.

MARK IS ANOTHER MEMBER OF TRANSFORMATION CHURCH, AND HE used to have a painful label stitched on his heart—"Orphan." The sense of belonging, of being part of a family, has an invaluable impact on our identities, and when that is missing, it can interfere with everything we try to do in life. Let me share Mark's story:

I was born in Liberia, and I lived there with my birth parents until I was seven. Then my dad took me to an orphanage started by African Christian Fellowship International (AFCI) because of the civil war in my country. I was taken to Daniel Hoover Children's Village outside of Monrovia, Liberia, in a town called Dixville. I do not know how long I stayed there. I just know it was a long time. I made new friends.

One of my friends was a drummer, and we would practice a lot in the orphanage. A crew of girls would always dance when we played drums. My friend and I would have to take turns playing drums because my hands would start to hurt. Our drums were actually a milk can.

I would get very sad when the rebels came to our orphanage and stole everything we had. They threatened to kill us and made us move out of the orphanage. This happened three times.

I thought I was going to die. I thought I was never going to have a real family. I did not like being an orphan.

ORPHANS FEEL ANONYMOUS

"Enough! I have been quiet about this topic for a long time. I cannot, nor will I, hold it in anymore!"

These words were the opening sentences in a response to a blog I had written where I called God "Papa." The rest of the response went like this: *"When people like you call God 'papa' or 'daddy', that can be extremely hurtful for people who have experienced abuse at the hands of their father. So, in the future, when you use the word 'papa' or 'daddy' for God, just know it can cause hurt."*

As the words of the person who identified him- or herself

as "anonymous" leapt off my computer screen into my heart, I realized that he or she had some deep daddy hurts.

I responded: "Anonymous, I have some father wounds too. So I feel what you are saying. I really do."

Then I wrote, "In the Gospels (Matthew, Mark, Luke, John), as well as in the apostle Paul's letters, Jesus and Paul both use the Aramaic word *Abba* to describe God the Father. The word *Abba* is equivalent to the English word *daddy* or *papa*. *Abba* is a term that paints a picture of the intimacy that God the Father desires with His children. *Abba* paints the picture of a tenderhearted, love-filled father reaching down to pick up and hug his child."

I closed with this: "Anonymous, I cannot and will not allow the pain of my past to murder the happiness I experience today from knowing God as my Papa."

Anonymous had allowed his or her daddy wounds to hide the beauty of experiencing God the Father as *Abba*. When you and I focus on how we've been done wrong in our past, we do not focus on how we've been done right by Jesus.

The word *anonymous* can be defined as lacking uniqueness or distinction. When we allow daddy wounds to limit our lives, we become anonymous people. When we are not connected to God our Father, we do not know who we are—we feel orphaned—and lose the capacity to discover our uniqueness. When we feel anonymous, we roam through life lost, looking for a love and an identity that no human, no job, no amount of money could ever provide.

Through years of discipleship and mentoring others, I have learned that the people who manage to climb out of emotional quicksand are those who intentionally stop the cruel, destructive habit of revisiting in their minds the events or the people who have hurt them. Instead, by an act of faith, they start the soul-healing habit of replaying in their minds the message that Jesus loves them, cares for them, was wounded for them, died to forgive them, and now makes His home in their hearts to live His beautiful life through them.

ORPHANS FEEL ABANDONED

My favorite color is yellow. That's because my dad bought me a yellow bike for my sixth birthday. He wasn't around much after that. As I said earlier, he and my mother were both teenagers when I was born, and things did not work out between them.

One of the proudest days of my life was in fifth grade, when I was playing flag football and I looked up into the stands and saw him there. His presence inspired me to put forth my best effort, and I ended up scoring the winning touchdown. My teammates picked me up on their shoulders and carried me off the field. That was an incredible, memorable moment, but what I really wanted was to hear what my dad thought.

Sadly, I do not remember what happened after that moment. Did he hug me and say, "Son, I am so proud of you"? Did we go eat greasy burgers afterward? I do not know. And I don't know why I cannot remember.

In eighth grade, my dad showed up with my mom at one of my basketball games. This time I was angry. I wondered, *Why show up now? Where have you been, Dad?* And to make matters worse, he was sitting next to my mom. My blood was boiling with anger!

He yelled at me the entire game. As I look back with a heart protected by Jesus and eyes that can now see my father's own wounded heart, I understand he was just trying to encourage his son. He was doing the best he could, but at that time I interpreted his encouragement through the ears of my pain.

I played terribly. But I thought the night of misery had ended. Little did I know it was about to get worse.

My dad walked into the locker room and began to talk with my basketball coach. It was clear to my coach and me that my father had an addiction issue. My coach and I made eye contact, then quickly pretended we had not. I was humiliated. At that moment, I committed to live as though my father did not exist. I was determined to show him I could make it without him.

And from that moment on, I began wearing a new label: "Orphan." I was fatherless.

MARINATE ON THAT!

My seventeen-year-old daughter, Presley, teaches me a lot about life. When I start to feel sorry for myself, she will say, "Dad, a *whambulance* is not coming to get you." What she's wisely telling me is this: "Stop feeling sorry for yourself!" And she's right. When we wallow in self-pity, the pain or event that caused the pain only gets worse. It magnifies.

And did you realize that whatever we magnify, we worship? And whatever we worship, we resemble? If we wallow in self-pity, we *will* become more pitiful and limit our lives. If we stay in Jesus and meditate on what He's accomplished on our behalf, we magnify His great work, and as we do this, we worship Him. The result is that daily we are transformed into His image, releasing His limitless life through us.

Presley is right. No whambulance is coming. But a Savior is. In fact, He already has. And He wants us to experience the love of His Papa.

ORPHANS FEEL AFRAID

When I was about three, I spent the night at my father's house in the Lincoln Heights Courts housing projects on the west side of San Antonio. I remember being abruptly awakened from my sleep. My father's dad had come home drunk. I can still recall the curse words that flew out of my grandfather's mouth like weapons. He cussed everyone out and threatened to kick us out of the house he "paid the bills for."

My father gently talked to his drunken, anger-filled father and restrained him. This was not the first time my dad had had to do this.

I do not know the backstory of why my grandfather was doing what he was doing, but I can now see that my dad had his own share of daddy wounds. He was a spiritual orphan too. During a conversation with my dad in August 2012, I asked him, "What was your relationship with your father like?"

He said, "My father worked all day and drank cheap wine all night. In a drunken rage he would then try to beat my mom. As I got older, I learned to calm him down and stop him. I never thought about hurting him because he was my father, and I loved him."

People live out of either the hurt they feel or the healing Jesus provides. Your parents will never be perfect. And you will never be a perfect parent. But there is a perfect God who, over time, will bring healing to hurtful circumstances.

I spent years being angry and bitter toward my father. These toxic emotions only limited my life. Do not let anger and bitterness limit you too. Our Papa in heaven is the only One who can provide us with the love and, ultimately, the identity we have been created for—a child of God.

Jesus paid too high a price for you, He sacrificed too much for you, and His victory is too great for you to be anonymous! We do not have to live as spiritual orphans anymore. Right now, God the Papa says, *I want to adopt you as My child. Will you let Me?*

Listen to His voice through the words of Paul the apostle: "God decided in advance to adopt us into his own family by bringing us to himself through Jesus Christ. This is what he wanted to do, and it gave him great pleasure. So we praise God for the glorious grace he has poured out on us who belong to his dear Son" (Eph. 1:5–6 NLT).

THE GOD WITHOUT LIMITS

GameChangers in More Than Sports

On May 24, 2012, at the request of my former high school coach, D. W. Rutledge, the executive director of the Texas High School Coaches Association, I participated in an event that I anticipate will change the trajectory of America, the inaugural "GameChanger Coaches Leadership Summit." Three hundred of the most influential high school coaches and administrators in the state of Texas were present. The theme of the leadership summit was "Impacting a Fatherless Generation." Here are some reasons why the summit was needed:[1]

Drug and Alcohol Abuse
- Fatherless children are at a greater risk of abusing drugs and alcohol.

Behavioral Disorders
- Eighty-five percent of all children who display behavioral disorders come from fatherless homes.

High School Dropout
- Seventy-one percent of all high school dropouts come from fatherless homes.

Prison
- Eighty-five percent of all youths locked up in prisons grew up in fatherless homes.

Teen Pregnancy
- Seventy-one percent of teenage pregnancies are to children of single parents. Daughters of single parents are 2.1 times more likely to have children during their teenage years than are daughters from intact families.

Youth Suicides
- Sixty-three percent of youth suicides are from fatherless homes.

Gender Confusion
- Boys who grow up in fatherless homes are more likely to have trouble establishing appropriate sex roles and gender identity.

Poverty
- Children in fatherless homes are five times more likely to live in poverty.

These are sobering statistics—40 percent of children in America will not have Dad at home.[2] And 72 percent of Americans feel that the greatest social problem in America is fatherlessness.[3]

Coach Rutledge asked me to speak on the topic "Can a Coach Change a Young Person's Life?" I did not have to prepare for this presentation because this presentation is my life.

There was not a dry eye in the auditorium.

> Coaches and administrators were inspired and challenged. They saw in me what they could be in the lives of the young men and women they coach and teach.
>
> As the executive director of the Texas High School Coaches Association, Coach Rutledge is always looking for ways to make a difference in a young person's life through the power of coaching and teaching.

TIME FOR A NEW LABEL . . . "ADOPTED"

Today my father and I are friends. Not too long ago, at a Cracker Barrel restaurant, he dazzled my children with his skills in a game of checkers. My son, Jeremiah, was impressed. "Dad, Grandpa is awesome at checkers. He is like a Jedi." I love my earthly papa, and he loves me.

How was I able to reach out to my father and restore our relationship? Truly it was through the grace of God. The keys to taking on the new label of "Adopted" are in the love God pours over us as His children.

Key 1: Embrace the Friendship of God

I don't want to imagine life without the coaches I had growing up—men like my football, basketball, and track coach in middle school. He was always a source of encouragement to me. He was the coach my dad talked to in the locker room that night so long ago.

Coach gave me permission to dream dreams I did not know were even possible. After practice one day, he told my mom, "If Dewey continues to work hard, he could get a football scholarship one day."

When Mom told me what he had said, I think I said something like, "What is a football scholarship?"

"It means you can go to college for free and play football!" she answered.

At that moment, in the fall of 1984, a tiny seed of a dream was planted in the soil of my heart. In the winter of 1989, that seed became a reality. Coach did something my father should have done: he inspired me to see a future that one day could be mine.

My football and basketball coach at Fox Tech High School in ninth and tenth grades always showed me favor. He treated me better than he did the other kids. Or at least I thought that. He probably made all the kids feel that they were his favorite. He'd give me rides home after practice. I loved that time with him because he would talk to me about life. And he would buy me dinner from McDonald's too. It feels good to know someone cares about you.

I loved Coach Mike Sullivan, my defensive back coach at Converse Judson High School, because he brought out the best of me. I also had a strong dislike for him because he brought out the best of me! The Converse Judson Rockets were one of the top five football programs in the state of Texas, and everything the Judson football program did was with "Rocket Pride." That meant excellence, sacrifice, teamwork, and hard work. New to the program, it was difficult for me to keep up the pace or the intensity of practice. I had never seen such excellence, which required my best every day.

Like a father, Coach Sullivan saw in me what I did not—greatness—but he drilled deep into my soul and ultimately unearthed my ability to become one of the greatest football players in Converse Judson history. He relentlessly pushed me to the brink of myself.

One day during my senior year at Judson, I decided to skip practice because I was now a team captain. I showed up the next day to find out that I'd lost my starting position. In the next game my team won 45-0 without me.

The following Monday, Coach Sullivan and I had what I now call "the talk." Through a waterfall of tears, he looked into my eyes, which were filling with tears as well. He said, "Dewey, you can be great! But I will not allow you to be just an average football player. If you are going to play for Judson, I demand your very best every day." Then he extended his hand toward mine, cupped it, and then clinched it into a fist and said, "Your future is in my hands. What are you going to do, son?"

The following day at practice, I had a new fire in my heart, a new energy, and a new passion for not just football, but life. I did not automatically get my starting position back. I was still not starting the next game. I thought my career was over. But after the first play of the game, Coach Sullivan said, "Dewey, get in!" When he called my name, I blasted onto the field like a Judson Rocket and destroyed the team we were playing. I went from being a good high school player to one of the best in the state of Texas! My career took flight and soared to places that ultimately led to the NFL.

Coach Sullivan was like a second father to me. He saw the greatness that was buried deep down within me, and he called it out of me by challenging me to step up and be a man. He loved me enough to push me further than I'd ever been pushed so I could go further than I ever thought was possible.

There is also Coach Rutledge, my high school football coach, the head football coach at Judson, and a legend in the football-crazy state of Texas. He has been inducted into numerous halls of fame and collected enough coaching awards to fill a big gym. But beyond all the state titles and accolades,

Coach is a great man who was a father to many young men like me who did not have fathers. He shaped my life more than any other man on earth. He had the unique ability to take the disciplines of football and show his players how to integrate those disciplines into the game of life. He stressed character development, sacrifice, teamwork, and work ethic. He wanted us to win on and off the field. And many of us have.

To this day, I'm in awe of Coach. As an impressionable teenager, I just wanted to be like him. I did not know what the "It" was he had; I just knew I wanted "It" too. The "It" that Coach had was a person—Jesus. Because I did not grow up in a Christian home, I had no idea what a Christ-follower was. I just knew I wanted to be like Coach Rutledge. He used to say that the football field was his pulpit and his teams were his congregation. He prayed for us before and after practice. I want to thank Coach for showing me honor, integrity, vision, and love.

Though he was not a coach, I am also thankful for my grandfather William E. Gilliam, who taught me what hard work was. I never saw him miss a day of work.

I am grateful for all these remarkable men who filled the void in my life as I was growing up, but I am even more grateful to God. I was able to finally reach out to my earthly father because God the Papa had reached out to me. That's what grace does. It pursues and reaches out to us—God's very own enemies—so friendship can be restored. God the Father reached out to me when I was not even thinking about Him.

Consider Romans 5:8–11:

> But God showed his great love for us by sending Christ to die for us while we were still sinners. And since we have been made right in God's sight by the blood of Christ, he will certainly save us from God's condemnation. For since

our friendship with God was restored by the death of his Son while we were still his enemies, we will certainly be saved through the life of his Son. So now we can rejoice in our wonderful new relationship with God because our Lord Jesus Christ has made us friends of God. (NLT)

God the Father desired to be my friend, and through the death and resurrection of His Son, I became His friend. When the friendship of God seized my heart, remaining unrestored to my father was no longer an option. It was an act of faith to reach out to my dad. It was hard, but it was so worth it! I no longer wanted to limit my life when the limitless love of God was available to me.

Key 2: Accept and Imitate the Forgiveness of God

I sat at my desk, staring at my computer screen, with a knot in my throat. I knew what I needed to do, but I was afraid to do it. I didn't want to do it either. I was typing letters to my friends and family members about my newfound faith in Jesus and how it was making me a new person. As I was talking about how forgiving, merciful, and loving Jesus was, the Holy Spirit was impressing on my heart that I needed to find and forgive my father.

I heard a voice. I do not know if it was God's voice or my voice. But I heard a voice. And the voice said, *Find your father.*

"No," I said, adding some curse words. "He was the one who abandoned me at the age of five! He was the one who decided to live a destructive life! He was the one who never came to my football games—not in middle school, not in high school, not in college, not even in the NFL!" As I sat at my desk, under the gracious conviction of the Holy Spirit, I finished with, "He hurt me! I will not find him."

Like the loving Papa that God is, I sensed Him whisper in my soul, *Son*, you *hurt* Me *with your sin, but I sent Jesus to find you. I'm rich in mercy, and I have made you alive with My Son, Jesus, so you can forgive your father.*

At that moment I had a choice: Would I live by faith or not? To live by faith meant that I would have to extend the same forgiveness to my father that Jesus had extended to me.

I made some phone calls to Texas. Eventually I found out he was in a Texas prison. I wrote him a short letter, seeking a relationship. The letter said, "Dad, I want you to know that I love you and forgive you. I want you to be a part of my life and my family's life. I want your grandchildren to know you."

I did not hear anything for several weeks. One afternoon I checked the mail, and buried under the mountain of magazines and other stuff I did not want to read was a letter from my father. A flood of emotions washed over me. I trembled as I opened the letter. Would he reject me? Would he be angry with me? Would he hurt me again?

Despite the tears that slightly blinded me, I read the words, "Son, thank you for forgiving me. I want to be a part of your life and my grandchildren's lives. I love you." That was the first time my father said "I love you" to me.

After my dad was released from prison, I was able to buy him some clothes so he could go job hunting. That felt really good.

I was able to reach out and forgive my father because God the Father reached out and forgave me. That's what grace does. It pursues and reaches out to sinners like me. In a violent act of holy justice and unconditional love on the cross, my past, present, and future sins were forgiven. Ephesians 4:32 says, "Be kind to each other, tenderhearted, forgiving one another, just as God through Christ has forgiven you" (NLT). Now I had to forgive my father in light of how God the Papa had forgiven me.

When I look back into the Derwin Gray files, I think, *How can God forgive a person like me?* And I hear God whisper, *How can I not forgive a person like you? You are exactly who I sent My precious Son to die for.*

When I forgave my father in response to my heavenly Father forgiving me, I escaped a dark prison cell of self-limitation. The prison doors are wide open! Jesus has paid the price and paved the way, so come on out of that dark prison cell of unforgiveness and walk in the light of freedom. It is time to forgive the person or persons who injured your heart.

Key 3: Accept the Adopting Love of God

One of my great pleasures in life is coaching and watching my son, Jeremiah, play football. God has blessed him with great ability, and I cannot imagine not watching my son play a game. I shared with you earlier that my father never attended one of my football games in middle school, high school, college, or the NFL. When I quiet my soul, I realize now that my heavenly Father was at every game, cheering for me and calling my name.

I was able to reach out and restore my relationship with my father because God is a "Father to the fatherless" (Ps. 68:5 NLT). Having God as my Father strengthened and filled my heart with love toward my earthly father. I can now see my father's pain. And not only is God my Papa, He has also adopted me into His family. Ephesians 1:5–6 tells us, "God decided in advance to adopt us into his own family by bringing us to himself through Jesus Christ. This is what he wanted to do, and it gave him great pleasure. So we praise God for the glorious grace he has poured out on us who belong to his dear Son" (NLT).

Please reread that passage slowly: it brings God pleasure to adopt spiritual orphans into His family. God smiles! He is happy! God is beside Himself with joy indescribable at the thought of adding sons and daughters to His family. He smiles because we are His children. Adoption into God's glorious family means that everything that Jesus has—His rights, His privileges—we now have because we belong to Jesus, the Father's Beloved. As this gospel truth moved from theory in my mind to conviction in my heart, it moved my hands to action. I had to find my father and restore my relationship with him.

JOINING THE BIGGEST AND BEST FAMILY OF ALL

I want to conclude this chapter with the rest of Mark's story.

After many years in the orphanage, I was adopted by the Covington family. When I heard that I got adopted, I freaked out! I was so excited. I was getting ready for church on a Sunday morning, and then I heard some of my friends coming into my dorm, calling my name, saying, "Mark, you're going to America. Get in the car."

And I was like, "Stop. Stop funning. That's not funny, you guys. That's not funny." And then they were like, "No, I'm serious. You're going to America. Pastor Kofi is here. Go get in the van." I'm like, "Oh, dude, I'm so excited. I'm going to America."

We got in the car and made a few stops. We stopped at a nice African clothing store so that we could get some nice clothes, not all the beat-up clothes I was used to wearing. And then when we got to America, we started taking the escalator. I took the stairs because I didn't know what it was. So I just took the stairs, and then I saw my mom and dad and my family. Well, I saw someone. I saw two families. So, I was like, "Which one's mine?" And then my mom was like, "Mark, over here." And I saw my dad standing there. He looked at me and he's like, "This is my son." Then I held my new sisters'—Emma's, Lucy's, and Gemma's—hands.

My new family kept saying, "Welcome; you're going to have a great life. You're going to have a future." I was smiling the whole time. It's like, yes! I'm happy. When I hear the word adopted now, all I hear is I have a family that loves me now.

I pray that when you, like Mark, hear that God the Papa has adopted you, you hear, "I am loved." You have a new label—adopted child of God.

See how very much our Father loves us, for he calls us his children, and that is what we are!

1 John 3:1 NLT

TRANSFORMATION MOMENT

Head

Out of an act of amazing grace that makes God the Father smile, you have been adopted into His family through the work of Jesus. Read 1 John 3:1; Ephesians 1:5–6; John 1:12; and Romans 8:15–17.

Heart

Pray:

Papa, today I choose to believe and receive the gospel truth that I have been adopted into Your family through the wonderful work of Your beloved Jesus. I am Your child. All that belongs to Jesus now belongs to me because I belong to Him. His inheritance is mine. I choose to never wallow in self-pity but to soak in the sweetness of soul-healing love. I am Your adopted child. Thank You.

Hands

- Reach out to the people you need to forgive. Write a letter. Make a phone call. Send a text. Extend an invitation. It's time to get released from the self-limiting prison cell of unforgiveness and walk in freedom.

FIVE

FROM DAMAGED GOODS
TO TROPHY OF GRACE

People are made to be loved and things are made to be used. The confusion in this world is that people are being used and things are being loved.

—Unknown

ISRAEL'S ETERNAL GOD AND KING WALKED ON EARTH AS A MAN NAMED Jesus. God the Son became human to do what humanity could not do on its own—restore damaged people to their original purposes. As Jesus walked the dusty Palestinian roads, He chose a group of damaged men to be His "disciples," or students. Jesus' crew consisted of a terrorist, a demon-filled nut job who would betray Jesus for money, a chronic denier, a doubting Thomas, a racist, and a tax collector. (In Jesus' day, the last of these was worse than being a child molester!) How is that for a group of damaged people?

Can you imagine the way people talked about Jesus and His disciples? "There goes Jesus. That boy is crazy! He thinks he is some kind of messiah. Surely he can't be! A messiah would never choose loser disciples like the ones he is walking around with."

People may have given up on you. But Jesus has not. As long as you have breath in your lungs, Jesus will not give up on you. Ever. The skeletons in your closet do not scare Him. Jesus is attracted to damaged people like you and me. I am writing this book because of the limitless lives those "loser" disciples lived—and that you can live too.

Maybe one day someone somewhere will talk about how you were once counted out and considered a loser—but then you met Jesus, and He unleashed His limitless life through you, and because of you, his or her life is eternally better.

As Jesus and His disciples were traveling to Judea from Galilee, Jesus, as He so often did, acted in a way that was utterly radical, inconceivable, and from many Jews' perspectives, even sinful. He took His disciples to Samaria.

The shortest route from Judea to Galilee would have been through Samaria. But at that time in history, Jews, and especially a rabbi like Jesus, would never have taken that shortcut because Samaria was a land filled with people who were ethnically a mixture of Jew, Roman, Phoenician, and Greek. The Jews did not travel that way because the Samaritans were considered unclean.

By the time Jesus walked on earth, the Jews and Samaritans had been in a centuries-old feud. They hated each other. And right in the midst of this great hate, Jesus planned to detonate a grenade of love. He proudly took His disciples right through the middle of this forbidden land.

Because of the loving nature of Jesus, He goes to undesirable places to meet unwanted, damaged people. And He will annihilate our stupid, dehumanizing barriers so these outcasts can be transformed into His trophies of grace. Jesus unifies that which man divides. Let Ephesians 2:14 seep into your heart: "For Christ himself has brought peace to us" (NLT). He united Jews and Gentiles into one people when in His own body on the cross, He broke down the wall of hostility that separated us.

Tired from the journey, Jesus took a break at Jacob's Well near the Samaritan town of Sychar. His disciples headed into Sychar to buy food. On a positive note, the very fact that these Jewish men went into a Samaritan town to buy some food is a sign of growth. Before they met Jesus, it is unlikely they would have entered that city. Their racism and religious bigotry would not have allowed them to do so.

Why would Jesus, a Jewish rabbi, take His disciples to a place where other Jews would never, ever go? Because damaged people attract the heart of God.

DAMAGED PEOPLE ATTRACT GOD'S HEART

While Jesus was resting at the well, a woman showed up to draw water. Since we are not given her name, I will call this woman Sammie. Sammie arrived at the well at noontime, having walked about a half mile from Sychar. It would not be wise to walk that far for only eight ounces of water, so Sammie was most likely carrying a pretty good-sized water jar. Her noon arrival strongly suggests she did not want to see the other women who also went to the well daily for water. In this hot desert climate, women would get water from the well in the morning or at night, when the temperatures were cooler.

Sammie went to the well when no other women would be there because she saw herself as damaged goods. Others in her community also saw her as damaged. She was a moral outcast among the Samaritans because of her past, and she was a moral outcast among many Jews because of her mere existence.

When Sammie looked in the mirror, she saw someone unworthy. And why wouldn't she? She had been divorced five times. In Sammie's culture, a rabbi would permit two divorces, maybe, but five was simply unimaginable.

There's more though. Sammie was also living with a man who was not her husband.

Not only did Sammie walk a half mile to the well with a heavy water jar; she also walked with a heavy heart. Maybe you have already made a judgment about Sammie—a floozy? a prostitute?

Most likely she was a victim, with a label that read "Damaged Goods" tattooed across her heart. In this culture, women could not just go get a job and provide for themselves. After five divorces, what upstanding man would want to marry and provide for her? Perhaps out of hunger she was forced to live with a man who was not her husband so she could survive. What other option did she have? What man wants to marry a woman who is damaged goods? Her life was limited. Until she met the One who is Limitless Life.

MARINATE ON THAT!

A woman was not allowed to ask for a divorce in this culture. Only men could. And if a woman was caught in the act adultery, she would have been stoned to death.

DAMAGED PEOPLE LOOK WHOLE IN GOD'S EYES

When the people in Sammie's community looked at her, they saw damaged goods. Imagine how dehumanizing it would be to think that every day people in your community looked at you with disdain. But, as Jesus saw her slowly walking toward the well where He was waiting, He saw what others did not see: a future trophy of His grace.

How do you and I look at damaged people? Do we look at them through the grace-colored eyes of Jesus, or the dehumanizing lenses of judgment? Sometimes I think Jesus would have been kicked out of many of our churches because of the damaged people He would bring to Sunday service. He would bring sex traffickers; HIV-infected IV drug users; greedy, Ponzi-scheming Wall Street investment bankers; adulterous politicians; crackheads; women who have had multiple abortions; alcoholics who cuss like pirates—and messed-up people like you and me.

As Jesus walked into our weekend services with His motley crew of damaged people, would we see potential trophies of grace? Or would we judge these people and pull back from them in disgust?

It is my prayer that our local churches will have the heart of Jesus for damaged people and be accused of loving the unlovable just as Jesus did. "The Son of Man came eating and drinking, and they say, 'Look at him! A glutton and a drunkard, a friend of tax collectors and sinners!'" (Matt. 11:19).

I pray that they will attract damaged people the way Jesus did. I can only imagine the joy in Jesus' heart as He saw Sammie walking toward Him, knowing that her life would be transformed forever by a conversation over a water cooler in the desert.

Before time began, Jesus had scheduled His appointment with Sammie and had seen her walking to Jacob's Well. Long before Eden, He saw Sammie's pain-filled face and wept. He also saw Sammie's future transformation—and smiled.

Jesus was relaxing at Jacob's Well as Sammie arrived. And a conversation that Jesus had been waiting to have from all eternity ensued.

I imagine, with a slight grin on His face, Jesus asked Sammie for a drink of water. Can you hear that sound? Listen carefully. That is the sound of Jesus breaking through a barrier.

In the first-century world of the Jews, a Jewish rabbi would not even talk to his wife and daughters in public. But here was Jesus, asking a Samaritan woman for a drink! This was just not supposed to happen! A rabbi talking to a Gentile dog! But Jesus did not play by man's limiting, hate-filled rules that created barriers between people. He played by the kingdom of God's law of love that obliterated man-made barriers.

THE GOD WITHOUT LIMITS

Wanda's Story: From Damaged to Devoted

I grew up in a Southern family that went to church pretty much every Sunday. And even though we were a very dysfunctional family Monday through Saturday, when we went to church on Sunday, we faked like everything was okay. In my youth group I always felt like a big disappointment to God. I was taught to live for Jesus but felt I always let Him down. I felt I could not show God the ugly and hurting parts of me. I learned at church that God was a judge waiting for me to screw up again. God was a critical, distant rule maker. I did not know that I could actually be known and loved by Jesus.

I stopped faking it when I went to college. I broke all God's rules. I felt as if I was in a prison, with no hope of ever measuring up to God's standards. I did not care about God anymore at that point. I hung with the other kids who were tired of faking it too. My new community accepted me as long as I partied, drank, got high, and had sex. I was searching for love and acceptance. I thought I could find it in the arms of a man. I totally screwed up my college career. I went to college as an honor society member with great grades but ended up failing out. I had to go home like a puppy with her tail between her legs. I had no clue what to do with my life. Then I found out I was pregnant.

I became a moral outcast—the person I was warned about in my church youth group. I did everything I was not supposed to do. And now I was living the consequences of it. When I went to the church I grew up in, I was totally rejected by everyone. On Sundays people would not even look me in the eyes, much less talk to me. My lifelong, childhood friends were told by their parents not to talk to or hang out with me. When I walked into the church, people would visibly turn around and walk away from me. Those kinds of reactions got worse the bigger my belly got. Even if I saw someone from my church out in public, they would act as if they did not know me. And these were people who had known me since fourth grade.

But God uses everything. And I think He can even use the judgment of people who don't even realize He's using them. He brought me to a place where I was so alone I really didn't have anybody to talk to—a place where the only person I could hear was Jesus. So, it was a really sweet time with Him, when He began to show me who He really was. Through this painful journey, He made it very clear to me that I was to place my baby up for adoption, and that He had a bigger plan for this baby.

Through that adoption process I met the family that eventually was going to raise the child I was carrying. It was a beautiful process even though it was really hard. It was also a time when the Lord began to show me who He was.

So much of the past couple of years has been a process of the Lord showing me why He has chosen to bless me in the way He has. I have an amazing husband I really love. And I'm blessed and grateful for this relationship. Through the years, the Lord has blessed us with four wonderful children.

What's been so beautiful about the journey that the Lord has had me on is with each child and with each relationship He has shown me that this is what He has for me. A lot of that has culminated with Transformation Church because this is a place that not only celebrates the good and the wonderful and the beautiful that God has created in each person, but they also celebrate the God who heals damaged people. They see that the brokenness is just the first step of the journey to grace. And I think that's one of the things that I love the most about the community of Transformation Church.

DAMAGED PEOPLE ARE HEALED BY GOD'S TOUCH

Sammie was shocked that a Jewish rabbi and enemy to the Samaritan people would ask her for a drink. In essence, Sammie would have thought, *Our people hate each other. Why would You ask me for anything?*

Jesus said, "If you only knew the gift God has for you and who you are speaking to, you would ask me, and I would give you living water" (John 4:10 NLT). Those words changed everything.

There are two important observations as we eavesdrop on this conversation.

1. God Has a Gift for Humanity

Grace is God's gift. A gift means you do not work to receive it. Grace is a gift that works for you.

"Now all glory to God, who is able, through his mighty power at work within us, to accomplish infinitely more than we might ask or think" (Eph. 3:29 NLT).

A gift by its very nature cannot be *earned* by good behavior. God's gift to humanity is earned by the perfect performance of Jesus.

> The sin of one man, Adam, caused death to rule over many. But even greater is God's wonderful grace and his gift of righteousness for all who receive it will live in triumph over sin and death through this one man, Jesus Christ. Yes, Adam's one sin brings condemnation for everyone, but Christ's one act of righteousness brings a right relationship with God and new life for everyone. Because one person disobeyed God, many became sinners. But because one other person obeyed God, many will be made righteous. (Rom. 5:17–19 NLT)

God's gift to humanity is not based on our goodness or lack of goodness, but based solely, entirely, and completely on God's goodness. God giving humanity a gift tears at the fabric of human existence. We humans are conditioned by our very nature to make people earn our love, and we, in turn, feel we have to earn someone else's love. God the Papa does not play by those rules. He gave humanity a gift despite our lack of goodness and poor performance.

In the exam of life, we have failed miserably. We scored 0. "But God showed his great love for us by sending Christ to die for us while we were still sinners" (Rom. 5:8 NLT). Despite our lack of goodness, God out of His unlimited goodness gave humanity a gift.

The Gift and the One who gave the Gift are the same. You cannot have one without the other. The Gift and Gift-giver are a package deal.

2. The Gift Was Israel's Messiah—Jesus Himself

Jesus offered Sammie that same gift.

The Gift That Keeps on Giving

When Jesus told Sammie that He could give her living water, Sammie, perplexed, asked Him, "How are You going to give me water? You do not even have anything to draw water from the well."

Jesus answered, "Everyone who drinks of this water will be thirsty again, but whoever drinks of the water that I will give him will never be thirsty again. The water that I will give him will become in him a spring of water welling up to eternal life" (John 4:13–14). Interestingly, in the Old Testament book of Jeremiah, God (YHWH) had described Himself as the fountain of living water (2:13 NLT).

I love how the Holy Spirit orchestrated this conversation between Jesus and Sammie. They were in a desert, during the hottest part of the day, and they were sitting at a well. Our very lives are like a desert; our souls are dry. No matter how much physical water we drink from the well, our lives are still spiritually parched and lifeless. No matter where we go, who we know, and what possessions we have, our souls are still eternally thirsty until we drink living water. And Jesus is that living water.

He is also eternal life: "This is what God has testified: He has given us eternal life, and this *life* is in his Son" (1 John 5:11 NLT, emphasis added). Eternal life is a person, not simply endless time or a destination one goes to when he or she dies.

As a pastor, I see so many Christ-followers struggling to grow as Jesus' disciples because they are waiting for eternal life in a future heaven instead of realizing, treasuring, and living from the gospel reality that eternal life means that the eternal Son of God eternally lives in them now to do and be everything God created them to be.

Water gives life. Since Jesus is the living water, He alone gives us His life for our life. He lives in us so we can live the life we could never live on our own.

Water also cleans. Sammie felt so dirty. But Jesus, the living water, washed her sins away. She was eternally forgiven, her sins forgotten by God for all time.

TIME FOR A NEW LABEL . . . "TROPHY OF GRACE"

Here are the keys to trading in your old "Damaged Goods" label for one that reads "Trophy of Grace":

Key 1: Drink God's Living Water

As Jesus was describing His living water, Sammie's curiosity was piqued, and she asked Jesus for a drink. But then Jesus seemed to switch gears by asking Sammie to go get her husband.

Can you imagine the look on her face when Jesus asked her to do this? The fear that spiked in her heart? She probably thought, *Here we go again. I knew once He found out how damaged I was, He'd reject me, like everyone else.* So Sammie sheepishly said, "I do not have a husband."

Jesus answered, "I know. You've had five husbands, and the man you are living with now is not your husband."

At this water cooler in the desert, the holy God of the universe and a sinful, moral outcast were together. And God did not condemn her. He showed her compassion, mercy, love, and grace. And yet, Jesus did not condone her sinful life. That's why He asked her to go get her husband. Would she be honest with Jesus? She was. This is *repentance*. Repentance is being honest with God about our sin and turning to Him.

The beauty of grace is that God already knows about our sin. He just wants us to be honest with Him and find healing and sin-overcoming strength in Him.

Religious people (notice I did not say gospel-centered people) have it all backward. They want to condemn and judge damaged people to repentance. "Stop doing what you are doing! Change your ways!" they say. But Jesus says, "I will change your ways by transforming your heart and giving you My living water to drink *so you can* stop doing what you are doing." Do you and I give people cups of grace to drink, or cups of judgment and condemnation?

Key 2: Believe Jesus When He Says, "I Am the Messiah"

As Jesus unfolded Sammie's not-so-pretty history right before her eyes, she realized she had been in conversation with the Messiah. The One she'd been waiting on was actually waiting on her at the well. Once it dawned on her that Jesus was the Messiah, she took off running back into the city of Sychar.

Here are three observations from this amazing exchange that reveal God's heart for damaged, hurting people:

First, Sammie left her water jar at the well! She had walked a half mile in the hot sun with a heavy water jar. But after she met Jesus, she left that jar at the well. Why? Because God used her physical need to show Sammie her spiritual need, Jesus. Her physical thirst was a symbol of her spiritual thirst that could only be satisfied by Jesus, who is a fountain of grace and life.

Second, she ran back to the very people she was trying to avoid. When we first met Sammie, she was avoiding the people of Sychar who knew her story. Shame had caused her to hide. But grace caused her to run to them so she could tell them about Jesus' story. Sammie didn't leave just her water jar at the well, she also left her shame and guilt.

I can hear Sammie running, saying, "I have met the Messiah! He knew how damaged I was, but He did not reject me! He offered me living water! I'm loved! If the Messiah can do this for me, He can do this for the people in Sychar too. Run, legs! Run! Go faster! I must tell them I have found the Messiah!"

Third, Sammie did what the disciples were supposed to do: tell the people of Sychar about Jesus. Can you imagine the thoughts going through the people of Sychar's minds? *Here comes Sammie. You know that poor girl has been divorced five times, and she's shacking up with the Roman soldier she met at the nightclub a few months ago.* Can you imagine their surprise when she started preaching Jesus to them?

This reminds me of one of my college buddies who knew me before I became a Christ-follower and found out I was now a pastor. He said to me, "Dewey, if you are a pastor, I will believe the Bible more. I have to!"

Sammie confidently, and with excitement bursting from every word, proclaimed to the people of Sychar, "Come and see a man who knew everything about me. Could this be the Messiah?" (John 4:29, paraphrased). And the people went out to meet Jesus, the Messiah.

One of the disturbing ironies of this story is that the disciples who were supposed to be telling the Samaritans about

Jesus did not. But a moral outcast did. Sammie, a brand-new convert to the faith, preached the gospel to the Samaritans, while the disciples, who had spent time in the greatest seminary ever—that is, their time with Jesus—did not. I wonder how many "good Christians" attend worship service after worship service and hear the gospel but never share it with people who have yet to receive Jesus as forgiver, healer, God, and King.

When I think of my life before Jesus, my heart breaks for people who were like me—insecure, fear-filled, and hellbound. I thank God that Transformation Church is one of the fastest-growing churches in America. My passion is not simply to grow a big church, however, but to be like Sammie and tell people about the One who knew all my ugly, dark sins and loved me anyway. Shame no longer limits me because Jesus' grace has liberated me.

Does the grace of Jesus compel you to share His story with damaged people? In light of all He has done for you, why not? "For the love of Christ controls us, because we have concluded this: that one has died for all, therefore all have died; and he died for all, that those who live might no longer live for themselves but for him who for their sake died and was raised" (2 Cor. 5:14–15).

Key 3: Embrace Jesus' Message: "I Am for All People"

As the disciples returned to meet Jesus at the well, they were stunned to see Him talking with a woman. I imagine they were thinking, *What kind of rabbi is this? First, he takes us to this God-forsaken place called Samaria, and now he is talking to a woman!*

The damaged and spiritually sick disciples were not only racist. They also had a bad case of sexism too. Despite the way they felt, they did not say anything to Jesus about it. Instead, the disciples wanted Jesus to eat, but He said, "My food is to do the will of him who sent me and to accomplish his work" (John 4:34). That is Jesus-speak for, "I have come to rescue the world! I am on a mission! *That* is My food!"

He continued, "Do you not say, 'There are yet four months, then comes the harvest?' Look, I tell you, lift up your eyes, and see that the fields are white for harvest" (v. 35). What in the world was going on? The disciples just wanted to give Jesus some food. Then Jesus went all cryptic on them!

In essence, Jesus was saying, "Gentlemen, you were just in a city full of people who do not know about Me and the salvation I freely offer. And you told no one!" Jesus used this illustration because His first-century world was agricultural. As Jesus was talking with His disciples, the backdrop was the city of Sychar, which is on a hill. The Samaritans dressed in all white. So Jesus was saying, "Fellas, look at the harvest that is dressed in all white. You just went into a city of damaged people, and you did not tell any of them about Me. They are ready to hear about Me, so I sent a damaged woman with a poor reputation to go and do *your* job."

Why didn't the disciples invite the people of Sychar to meet Jesus? They failed to share Jesus with the Samaritans because racism is a hard sin to break! The disciples' prejudices had conditioned them to only reach out to people who were like them, Jews. By Jesus' talking to a Samaritan woman, He was showing them that His kingdom was open to all who were willing to repent and receive Him.

REACHING THE *EVERYONE*—WHY ARE WE CALLED TO DO IT?

Is the church in America like the disciples? Do we only want to reach out to people who look like us, vote like us, or are of the same socioeconomic status as us? Is that why we have black churches, white churches, Latino churches, and Asian churches? In fact, the most segregated institution in America is the church of the living God.

While meeting with a group of pastors at Leadership Network in Dallas, Texas, our hearts were shattered as we discussed these sad, gospel-reducing statistics:

- Ninety-three percent of all churches are ethnically (racially) segregated.
- Churches in America are ten times more ethnically segregated than their neighborhoods and twenty times more ethnically segregated than their schools.

We have been conditioned to only reach people who are like us. Perhaps you are thinking, *Why does ethnic diversity in the local church matter?* It matters to Jesus because it displays the church's unity, which helps unbelievers realize that Jesus really did come to rescue the world. Jesus said, "I do not ask for these [His disciples] only, but also for those who will believe in me through their word, that they may all be one, just as you, Father, are in me, and I in you, that they also may be in us, so that the world may believe that you have sent me" (John 17:20–21). And multiethnic local churches give a beautiful picture of the future church in eternity:

> After this I looked, and there was an enormous crowd—no one could count all the people! They were from every race, tribe, nation, and language, and they stood in front of the throne and of the Lamb, dressed in white robes and holding palm branches in their hands. They called out in a loud voice: "Salvation comes from our God, who sits

on the throne, and from the Lamb!" All the angels stood round the throne, the elders, and the four living creatures. Then they threw themselves face downwards in front of the throne and worshipped God, saying, "Amen! Praise, glory, wisdom, thanksgiving, honour, power, and might belong to our God for ever and ever! Amen!" (Rev. 7:9 GNT)

THE STORY BEHIND THE STORY

Sammie the Samaritan woman was a Jew and a Gentile in one body. This is an awe-inspiring picture of the ethnic diversity that local churches are to have. How do we know? Am I making this up? Let's read Ephesians 2:14 (NLT) and 3:4–6:

> For Christ himself has brought peace to us. He united Jews and Gentiles into one people when, in his own body on the cross, he broke down the wall of hostility that separated us.

> When you read this, you can perceive my insight into the mystery of Christ, which was not made known to the sons of men in other generations as it has now been revealed to his holy apostles and prophets by the Spirit. *This mystery is that the Gentiles are fellow heirs, members of the same body, and partakers of the promise in Christ Jesus through the gospel.* (emphasis added)

Jews are people who are ethnically Jewish. And Gentiles are everyone else in the world. The local churches in Ephesus to whom Paul wrote were ethnically diverse during the first century because of the power of the gospel.

I believe one of the reasons the first-century church transformed the Roman world was because of the birth of multiethnic local churches comprised of Jews and Gentiles. In that time, this simply should not have been possible. Many Jews considered Gentiles to have been created as firewood for hell. In the first century, it was even unlawful for a Jewish man to help a Gentile woman in labor because that would help bring another worthless Gentile into the world. If a Jew even touched a Gentile, he would consider himself unclean.

It was in this racially turbulent world that "Christ . . . brought peace to us. He united Jews and Gentiles into one people when, in his own body on the cross, he broke down the wall of hostility that separated us. . . . Together as one body, Christ reconciled both groups to God by means of his death on the cross, and our hostility toward each other was put to death" (Eph. 2:14, 16 NLT).

The first-century Roman world must have looked in awe as Jews and Gentiles, who formerly hated each other, were now worshiping Jesus together, living in multiethnic community together, and going on missions together for the sake of the gospel. This miracle, in light of the extreme hatred between Jews and Gentiles, could only be explained by the resurrection of Jesus.

I wonder how America would be transformed by the power of the gospel if we allowed the gospel to once again create local churches filled with people from different ethnic and socioeconomic backgrounds?

AND THEY BELIEVED

As the result of a damaged woman who had encountered Jesus and shared Him, her fellow Samaritans said to her, "It is no longer because of what you said that we believe, for we have heard for ourselves, and we know that this is indeed the Savior of the world" (John 4:42).

What happened? The Samaritans saw a woman who was damaged goods be transformed into a trophy of grace. For all eternity Jesus will point to Sammie and proclaim to the entire universe, "Look at what I did! Look at My trophy of grace!" And He will say that about you, too, "So God can point to us in all future ages as examples of the incredible wealth of his grace and kindness toward us, as shown in all he has done for us who are united with Christ Jesus" (Eph. 2:7 NLT).

Wanda was labeled as damaged goods. Her life was limited. But because of Wanda, who has infused compassion into Transformation Church's outreach into our community, we have an incredible ministry in local public schools. We feed more than a hundred poverty-stricken kids every week during the school year through a backpack meal ministry. Many of the children we serve through this ministry do not eat healthy meals over the weekend. The love that transformed Wanda from damaged goods to trophy of grace is now touching countless lives in our public schools.

One Sunday morning I talked about how we feed children through our backpack ministry. Afterward, a mother came up to me and said, "I had no clue where my nine-year-old son was getting his backpack filled with food until I came to church this morning." She hugged me and sobbed, "Thank you." The entire family was baptized at Transformation Church on Easter 2012.

TRANSFORMATION MOMENT

Head

God is not intimidated by our damaged-ness; as a matter of fact, He is attracted to broken, damaged lives. From all eternity, He's looked forward to when His grace would encounter you. You are a trophy of Jesus' grace. This is an unchanging fact based on the unchanging character of God and grace of Jesus (Eph. 2:7).

Heart

Pray:

Lord Jesus, thank You for running toward me when others ran away from me. Thank You for not being repulsed by my damaged life. I am so thankful that on the cross You took my damages and shame. I choose to worship You by seeing and believing that I am Your trophy of grace. Thank You, Jesus.

Hands

- Who are the Samaritans in your life? Who are the people of different ethnic backgrounds with whom you normally would not share the life-transforming, damage-healing love of Jesus? Ask Him to give you His heart for people different from you and to empower you to break down barriers that divide humanity.

SIX

FROM RELIGIOUS TO GRACE-COVERED

For from his fullness we have all received, grace upon grace.

—John 1:16

I'M NOT A FAN OF RELIGION.

I wasn't honest enough with that last sentence. I profoundly dislike religion. However, I profoundly *love* religious people. Let me explain what I mean.

I define religion as humanity's attempt to reach up and earn God's acceptance, love, and blessings through good behavior or by keeping a specific set of religious principles or laws.

In the historic biblical Christian context, this is called "works-based righteousness." The religionist says, "If I can just be good enough, if I can just follow these principles and laws, I will become righteous enough. Then God will accept me; then God will love me; then God will bless me." Works-based righteousness produces performance-based living, which suffocates our souls. It's limiting.

Perhaps this illustration will help express my thoughts. Religion, or works-based righteousness, paints a picture of a god sitting atop a high peak, waiting for us to scale the mountain through our good behavior or adherence to a set of specific religious principles. The more "good" we do—keep the Sabbath, journey to a holy city, read the Bible, tithe, share our faith, and serve in the church—the closer we come to approaching our god through our good deeds.

If we do something bad, however, the god on top of the mountain turns Zeus-like and throws a lightning bolt to strike us and knock us back down the mountain. After the electric shock wears off and our singed hair stops smoking, we dust ourselves off, pull ourselves up by our bootstraps, and start the long trek all over again.

RELIGION ISN'T GRACE-FULL

As I was writing this chapter from my favorite coffee shop, a member of Transformation Church walked in and saw me staring at a blank computer screen. I had no idea how I was going to start this chapter until she showed up and encouraged me. With a Puerto Rican accent, she excitedly said, "Pastor, I love you. You have helped me and my family so much. I wrote you a letter." Her letter clearly demonstrates the stark contrast between an experience of true grace and the unfortunate contamination that the poisonous effects of religion have on so many Christians.

Dear Pastor Derwin,

Just a quick note to thank you for blessing my family every week! Even though I grew up in a Christian home and attended a private Christian school from kindergarten through high school, I have learned more about God and His grace through Transformation Church in the last two years than in the previous forty years I've been a Christian. I feel that every single week the sermon was written for ME.

First, I have learned how much God loves me. Throughout my Christian life, I was never sure if I did enough good things for God to love me. I thought God was up there in heaven with a belt ready to spank me every time I messed up. I now have a passionate relationship with Jesus! He is the One who is making me a better wife and mother! And my three teenagers love Transformation Church! Thank you for bringing the reality of Jesus and His grace to us in such a practical way.

Sadly, throughout my fifteen years of walking with Jesus, I've run across many Christ-followers suffocating in the carbon monoxide of religion instead of living from Jesus' accomplishments—His perfect life on our behalf, His death on the cross in our place, His resurrection from the dead, and His exaltation to the right hand of His Father as our advocate. Many Christ-followers try to live *for* God's acceptance, love, and blessings instead of living *from* God's love, acceptance, and blessings to us based on Jesus' accomplishments for us. Let the floodgates of God's grace sweep you off your feet:

All praise to God, the Father of our Lord Jesus Christ, who has blessed us with every spiritual blessing in the heavenly realms because we are united with Christ. Even before he made the world, God loved us and chose us in Christ to be holy and without fault in his eyes. God decided in advance to adopt us into his own family by bringing us to himself through Jesus Christ. This is what he wanted to do, and it gave him great pleasure. So we praise God for the glorious grace he has poured out on us who belong to his dear Son. (Eph. 1:3–6 NLT)

Right before Jesus died for the sins of the world, He uttered the words that every human heart was designed to hear: "It is finished." Those words meant that Jesus had accomplished everything that was needed to reconcile God to humanity and even to restore all creation.

RELIGION ISN'T GRACIOUS

When we live by religion, or works-based righteousness, we are never sure when God is pleased with our behavior. We are never certain that we are loved. How do you know when you've been good enough if His acceptance of us is based on our behavior?

The motivating fuels to keep climbing the high mountain are fear, shame, and guilt. This toxic soup produces a spiritual Ebola virus that slowly and painfully kills us. Sadly, religion produces both pride and despair. Pride says, "Look what I've done to earn God's acceptance, love, and blessings." Despair says, "I'm tired of trying to live up to God's standard. I give up! I can't keep the rules."

Pride produces spiritually arrogant people who look down on others who haven't climbed the stairway to heaven as high as they have. Judgmental attitudes and condemnation accompany them the way a nose accompanies a face. Pride also produces people who hide their sins from God and others. When you live a performance-based life, you enter into a false "spiritual identity protection program." The religious person has an image to protect because he wrongly believes that God accepts, loves, and blesses him based on his behavior. If your behavior does not live up to the standard, then God and people will reject you.

Some of the deepest, darkest sin issues I have counseled people through have been with longtime churchgoers. When you don't realize that Jesus *is* the basis of acceptance before God, you hide or protect your image through deception. If you come clean with your issues, the jig is up and you are found out as not being perfect. The gospel of grace informs us that Jesus went to the cross fully knowing our issues and imperfections. And on the cross He died for all our sins—the past ones, the present ones, and the future ones.

I no longer have to hide my sins, because God the Father's acceptance and love for me is based solely and completely on Jesus. I'm *in* Him. And the more I realize this gospel truth, the less I sin and the more I grow up as a follower of Christ.

In the garden of Eden, Adam and Eve hid when they sinned. Their nakedness was symbolic of their sin being exposed. Immediately after sinning, they covered themselves with fig leaves. This is symbolic of religion. Religion says, "You have sinned! You had better go and cover yourself up so you can be accepted by God." Grace says, "You can't cover up your sin no matter how hard you try. But God, who is good, will cover, forgive, and forget your sin for you as a gift." Check out Genesis 3:21: "And the LORD God made clothing from animal skins for Adam and his wife" (NLT).

In the garden, religion and grace presented themselves early in human history. Adam chose religion: "I will cover my sin myself." God chose grace: "Children, I will cover your sin as a gift."

This picture of God sacrificing an animal and clothing

Adam and Eve with the hide made from that sacrificed animal was a precursor to what Jesus would do for all humanity. Think about Galatians 3:27: "You were baptized into union with Christ, and now you are *clothed*, so to speak, with the life of Christ himself" (GNT, emphasis added).

Religion says, "Clothe yourself." Grace says, "God will clothe you with His precious Son, Jesus." Religion says, "Hide your sin." Grace says, "God hides us in His Son." "Your real life is hidden with Christ in God" (Col. 3:3 NLT). If you are a follower of Jesus, your acceptance, God's love for you, and every spiritual blessing you receive are totally, unequivocally, and solely because you are clothed in Jesus.

It's time for us to wake up to grace and the limitless life that awaits.

RELIGION MISSES THE MARK

I'm going to share a secret with you. I wish I could sing on the Transformation Church Worship Team. Seriously, I wish I could sing, but when God was handing out gifts, He handed me a football, not vocal cords that make sounds that harmonize.

Sometimes I really think I can sing. I'll listen to the late Sam Cooke, Israel Houghton, or Charlie Hall, and I think I can sound like them. Then I open my mouth and I sound nothing like them. I totally miss the mark.

That's the idea of sin—*missing the mark*. God has a mark or bull's-eye for humanity. And that bull's-eye is Jesus. Jesus is what God had in mind when He created humanity. Adam was the blueprint, but he blew it in the garden, so Jesus—God the Son—put on human flesh to show humanity what we were meant to be.

Jesus lived a perfect life for thirty-three years. Not only

did He obey the Ten Commandments perfectly, He also embodied them perfectly. He was truly alive as humanity was meant to be. In Jesus, we get a glimpse of what we will be like for all eternity. And what does His perfect life look like?

Awake and Alert

A few years back, my family and I, along with some friends, went to the Dominican Republic for vacation. We love the Dominican Republic. The culture is rich and diverse. The food is phenomenal. And the coffee is very, very special.

I'm a coffee drinker. I love the smell and the bold taste of black coffee. In the Dominican Republic, I met my favorite coffee over breakfast. As I lifted the cup toward my mouth, the rich, bold smell wrapped itself around my nose. I could taste its strong flavor even before it danced on my tongue. Man, I enjoyed that coffee.

In about ten minutes, something happened to me. A surge of energy filled my body, and before I knew it, I was wide-awake! I could hear and see everything. I told my wife, "Baby, I'm going running!" And I ran and ran and ran. The Dominicans and the other tourists must have thought I was a black Forrest Gump! Before that cup of Dominican coffee, I was sleepwalking.

MARINATE ON THAT!

I wonder how many people are sleepwalking through life? It is so limiting when we simply go through the motions and kind of just exist. Life is too short and you are too valuable to sleepwalk through life. It's time to wake up to the limitless life God has for you. Future generations are calling your name. They are pleading with you to wake up because the life you live today will affect their tomorrow.

In the Bible, the term *sleep* is used for both physical and spiritual death. Spiritual death means that humanity is severed from the life of God. According to the Story of Jesus, every human is a *spiritual stillborn*; we are dead men and women walking. This is humanity's ultimate problem, and it cannot be cured by religion. Religion cannot raise a spiritually dead man to life. Religion's attempt to wake up a dead man is like putting makeup on a corpse and expecting the corpse to live again.

Never, ever forget this: *Jesus did not come to earth on a rescue mission to make bad people good. He came to earth to make dead people alive through the gift of Himself.*

AIMING AT THE RIGHT TARGET

Dogs bark, eagles fly, and fish swim because it is in their nature to do those things.

Why does a human sin? He sins because humans are a spiritually dead race. When humans sin, we are simply being what we are by nature. Ephesians 2:1–3 describes the human condition outside of Jesus as dead in our sins, following demonic forces, and being under God's wrath because of our sin nature.

You may find this hard to believe, but I have never said to my children, "Presley and Jeremiah, you guys are perfect! Could you just sin once, please?" Why do we have to teach children to share, to love, and to be kind? We have to teach these positive character traits because kids are spiritually dead sinners by nature.

We are in need of a new nature—one that is not corrupted by sin. And there is only one life in the universe that is not corrupted with sin: Jesus'. And He wants to impart that incorruptible, immortal life to us. "Your new life is not like your old life. Your old birth came from mortal sperm; your new birth comes from God's living Word. Just think: a life conceived by God himself!" (1 Peter 1:23 MSG).

One of the many miracles of grace is that the very same Jesus who lived and embodied the Ten Commandments perfectly for thirty-three years on planet Earth now wants to take up residence in us and live that same life in and through us. Feast your eyes on this limitless truth: "To them God chose to make known how great among the Gentiles are the riches of the glory of this mystery, *which is Christ in you*, the hope of glory" (Col. 1:27, emphasis added).

Did you catch the reason the limitless life awaits you? "Christ in you, the hope of glory." Grace is not only all about Jesus—grace *is* Jesus. Can you imagine living a life loving God and loving your neighbors as yourself every day, all day? Sin is the failure to be what we ought to be and could be. But Jesus came to earth on a mission trip to show us who we ought to be. Then He died and rose again so we could be what God originally intended us to be—without limits.

HITTING THE BULL'S-EYE

In Ephesians 2:4–7, we learn that God is rich in *mercy*, is unequaled in His *love* for humanity, has made us *alive* together with Jesus, and shows us off like a proud father for all eternity as a testament to His amazing grace. Mercy is to the soul what water is to a thirsty man. Love is to the heart what oxygen is to the lungs. Life is to the body what food is to the stomach. Humanity is in need of mercy, love, and life. Religion can't provide these. Only Grace can because Grace is a person named Jesus.

Like the majority of Americans today, I didn't grow up in church. I didn't read the Bible. I was what pastors call "unchurched." I came to faith in a very unusual way in a very unusual place.

In 1993, the Indianapolis Colts drafted me to play football. My dream of playing in the NFL had come true. Little did I know, God was using the Colts organization as a means to an end, and that end was for me to know His Son, Jesus.

But before I get to my story of how God transformed my life, I must share with you someone else's story. My story wouldn't be without his. His name is Steve Grant.

THE GOD WITHOUT LIMITS

Grace in the Strangest Places

Steve's Story of Grace

Steve Grant grew up in a poverty-stricken, drug-infested neighborhood in Miami, Florida. His father deserted him when he was four, and his mother and grandmother did their best to raise him. He often says, "When I needed to know how to be a man, a man was nowhere to be found." He grew up angry, and that anger fueled him to excel in sports, so much so that he received a football scholarship to West Virginia University.

During his first two years of college, he enjoyed the perks of being a college football player. His primary focus was making it to the NFL so he could take care of his mother and grandmother. However, something began to happen his junior year in college.

A particular gentleman involved in a campus ministry was unrelenting in inviting Steve to a Bible study on campus. As Steve says, "Either someone gave him my class schedule or God was setting me up." After several months of being asked, Steve finally gave in and said he would attend, just to get this Christian off his back.

When Steve showed up for the first Bible study, he planned to stay sixty seconds but noticed that the head football coach for West Virginia was in attendance, so Steve marched to the front of the room and said, "Steve Grant here, Coach. I just wanted you to know."

Steve came to the Bible study for three straight weeks, each time sitting in the front row, next to the head coach. On the fourth week, Steve showed up only to discover the head coach was not there in his usual seat in the front row. Immediately he wanted to leave, but he was trapped up front and could not make an unnoticed exit. While Steve sat up front, not really wanting to be there, God's grace began to melt Steve's hard, angry heart. As he explains, "All the things my grandmother used to tell me as a little boy about Jesus and His grace began to break through and soften my hard heart."

During a conversation with the gentleman who invited Steve to the Bible study, the man told him, "You are getting ready to go to the NFL and make millions of dollars. But that does not make you successful. What makes a man successful is when he bows his knee to Jesus and receives Him as His God and King and lives for His glory."

After this conversation, Steve called his grandmother crying, saying, "Granny, I just gave my life to Jesus."

On the other end of the line was dead silence. And then his grandmother said, "Baby, I've been praying for you to give your life to Jesus ever since you were born."

With his newly found life and passion, Steve told God, "Please do not let me get drafted by the Indianapolis Colts or the

Green Bay Packers." When the Indianapolis Colts drafted Steve in the 1992 NFL draft, he said he had one goal: "To win as many of my teammates to Jesus as possible!"

My Story of Grace

The God who is rich in mercy and filled with love unending sent Steve Grant to the Indianapolis Colts as a missionary to introduce me and many of my teammates to Jesus. When I first met Steve, I knew him by another name: *the Naked Preacher*!

As soon as I got to the Colts in 1993, I noticed a linebacker on the team who would take a shower, dry off, wrap a towel around his waist, and then pick up his Bible and ask those of us in the locker room a bizarre question: "Do you know Jesus?"

And, I thought, *Do you know you are half-naked?!*

I asked the veterans on the team, "What's up with the half-naked black man walking around talking about, 'Do you know Jesus?'?"

They said, "Don't pay attention to him. That's the Naked Preacher."

At this point in my life, I did not want anything to do with Jesus or a half-naked black man talking about Him, so I tried to avoid him.

One day after practice, I was sitting at my locker and I saw the Naked Preacher walking toward me. "Rookie D. Gray, do you know Jesus?" I tried to pretend I didn't hear him, and I turned my back and ignored him.

He repeated the question, but this time he was at my locker.

Even though I was not a churchgoer or involved in any religious group, I gave what I thought was a very religious answer: "I'm a good person." I explained to him that I was the only male in my family over the age of twenty who had not been to jail, who did not have a substance abuse problem, who had graduated from high school and college, and who did not have a child outside of marriage.

Steve opened up his Bible and shared two verses with me: "And Jesus said to him, 'Why do you call me good? No one is good except God alone'" (Luke 10:18) and "For all have sinned and fall short of the glory of God" (Rom. 3:23). Steve explained that according to the Bible, only God is good; everyone else has sinned and falls short of God, who is the standard of goodness and righteousness. This disturbed me!

So I said, "Naked man, are you telling me that my comparison is God and not other people?"

He said, "Yes."

"God is perfect! What can I do to be perfect?"

He answered, "Nothing."

I said, "I'm in big trouble."

"Rookie D. Gray," he said, "now you are starting to get it. You can't do anything to reach a perfect God. But Jesus has done everything for the perfect God to come down and reach you."

I sat in silence. It was as if my eyes and ears were suddenly opened. That conversation began a friendship that continues to this very day.

Over the next five years, I watched Steve share the gospel by living it. When my teammates needed advice, they were at the Naked Preacher's locker, seeking wisdom. He was involved in the community of Indianapolis, always giving his money and time to make someone else's life better. He displayed Jesus in the way he loved his wife and children. He preached through his words and actions. As the Naked Preacher preached, God's love crushed me.

I achieved the American Dream only to realize it could not

give me the power to love my wife or forgive my father. My fame and money could not help me get rid of my shame, guilt, fear, and insecurity. And during the years of 1995–1997, I started getting injured on the football field. As a football player, my body was my god. My body was how I made my living. As my body began to give out, I was stripped of everything I thought gave me meaning. I was left with nothing even though I seemingly had everything.

On August 2, 1997, after lunch at training camp with the Indianapolis Colts, I was walking to my dorm room at Anderson University in Anderson, Indiana. Once I got to the room, I picked up the phone and called my wife, and said, "I want to be more committed to you. And I want to be committed to Jesus."

At that moment I realized that God loved me. Not because I could run fast or jump high or because I was good, or even for what I could give Him. I realized that as Jesus hung on the cross, I was forever loved and accepted by God. For the first time in my life, I knew I mattered and that I would not ever be abandoned again. At that moment, I believe I was "saved."

Here are the keys to exchanging your "Religious" label with one that reflects grace:

Key 1: Know That You Have Past Grace

Repeat after me: *"I have been saved from the penalty of sin"* (justification).

So, what does the word *saved* mean, anyway? The Greek word used for "salvation" in the Bible is *sozo*. "Salvation," or *sozo*, in the New Testament indicates that we have been saved from the penalty of sin in the *past*, that we are being saved from the power of sin in the *present*, and that we will be saved from the presence of sin in the *future.* Just as God is triune—the Father, the Son, and the Spirit—salvation is also triune—past, present, and future. The first stage is called *justification.*

Follower of Jesus, in the past you were declared to be as righteous as Jesus Himself.

On August 2, 1997, I experienced that first stage of salvation. Through faith in Jesus, God the Father *justified* me; that is, He declared me to be the very righteousness of Jesus. That's the only way I, or anyone, could be restored to friendship with God the Father. On the cross, God the Papa exchanged all my unrighteousness for all Jesus' righteousness. From that moment forward and for all eternity, when God the Father sees me, He sees me robed in the very righteousness of Jesus. Not only am I completely forgiven by God, I am the very righteousness of His Son, which makes me totally pleasing to God the Father.

How ridiculous and glorious is this gospel reality? No wonder it's called good news!

This is totally unfair. And by the way, we don't want "fair" anyway. What we want is grace. Look at Romans 3:24 and Philippians 3:7–9 with eyes of faith:

[We] are *justified by his grace as a gift*, through the redemption that is in Christ Jesus. (emphasis added)

I once thought these things were valuable, but now I consider them worthless because of what Christ has done. Yes, everything else is worthless when compared with the infinite value of knowing Christ Jesus my Lord. For his sake I have discarded everything else, counting it all as garbage, so that I could gain Christ and become one with him. I no longer count on my own righteousness through obeying the law; rather, I become righteous through *faith* in Christ.

For God's way of making us right with himself depends on *faith*. (NLT, emphasis added)

Please understand and lock this truth deep in your heart and throw away the key: God the Papa only accepts one person in the entire universe, His beloved Son, Jesus. But because you and I are "in" Jesus, He accepts us and sees us as righteous. Therefore we do not need to strive or struggle to earn God's love, acceptance, or forgiveness.

Why? Because we are in Christ, who is our righteousness! "Because of him [God] you are in Christ Jesus, who became to us wisdom from God, righteousness and sanctification and redemption, so that, as it is written, 'Let the one who boasts, boast in the Lord'" (1 Cor. 1:30–31).

My friend, you are the supreme object of God the Father's affection because you are "in" His beloved Son, Jesus. We can eternally stand before God the Father with smiles on our faces because our acceptance and righteousness have been given to us as gifts birthed out of unconditional love.

"Therefore, since we have been justified by faith, we have peace with God through our Lord Jesus Christ. Through him we have also obtained access by faith into this grace in which we stand, and we rejoice in hope of the glory of God" (Rom. 5:1–2).

The reality of being declared "righteous" transformed my life. As this gospel truth began to wallpaper my mind and penetrate my heart, it transformed how I saw myself.

I began to see what God saw. I no longer wanted to intentionally act in ways that did not reflect who God saw me as, the very righteousness of Christ. It was not religion that transformed me. It was the overwhelming reality that grace was stunning and more gorgeous than I ever imagined.

Let the sweetness of Ephesians 2:8–9 satisfy your soul:

"For by grace you have been saved through faith. And this is not your own doing; it is the gift of God, not a result of works, so that no one may boast."

Religion says, "Do something to earn God's acceptance, love, and blessings." Grace says, "Jesus has done everything so that God can accept, love, and bless you." Our role is to believe grace (Jesus), receive grace (Jesus), and live through grace (Jesus).

Perhaps you are saying, "Pastor Derwin, are you telling me that I can do whatever I want, and because I have faith in Jesus, God the Father still sees me as righteous even if I'm unrighteous?" *Yes.* And here's the beauty of grace: when your heart is overrun by the gospel of grace and you realize that your failures and sins do not prevent God from seeing you as righteous, then you will not want to act in unrighteous ways. People who get grace go further and grow faster in the kingdom because they are living *from* God's acceptance, love, and blessing.

Key 2: Know That You Have Present Grace

Now repeat this: "*I am being saved from the power of sin in the present*" (sanctification).

The second stage of salvation is called *sanctification*, which is salvation from the present *power* of sin. Justification is the *past* act, where God the Papa declares His children to be righteous in Christ, while sanctification is the *present*, life-long, continual process by which God the Spirit transforms us into Jesus' image.

Our actions begin to display in the present what we are by our position in Christ. "And we all, with unveiled face, beholding the glory of the Lord, are being transformed into the same image from one degree of glory to another. For this comes from the Lord who is the Spirit" (2 Cor. 3:18).

Please remember our justification is the basis of our

sanctification. Sanctification is not the basis of our justification.

Follower of Jesus, in this present moment, through the Spirit's presence and power, you are being transformed into the image of Jesus.

But She's White. But He's Black

I'm from San Antonio, Texas. My wife, Vicki, is from Darby, Montana. San Antonio is urban, and Darby is rural (it doesn't even have stoplights). I'm black. Vicki is white. We met in 1990 at Brigham Young University. I was there on a football scholarship. Vicki was there on academic and track scholarships. We met on January 15, 1990. A year and half later, we were at the jewelry store buying an engagement ring.

The first time I brought Vicki home to San Antonio to meet my family, my grandmother, who basically raised me, did not like the idea of us being engaged. She said, "I want black grandbabies!" My heart was crushed. She did not like the idea of me marrying Vicki because she was white. This is racism. And racism is a sin.

But here's the deal: My grandmother was born in the 1930s in San Marcos, Texas, under Jim Crow laws. Her experience growing up in Texas was dehumanizing and brutal. Her interactions with white people were not very positive. She saw Vicki through the filters of hurt and pain at the hands of white people. But Jesus transforms us to see people through the filter of His love.

When Vicki brought me home to meet her mom and stepfather, they did not want us to get married either. The problem was that I was black. Vicki's stepfather had had some bad experiences with black people in the military, so he viewed me through the filters of his hurt and pain, but Jesus transforms us to see people through the filter of His love.

And that's exactly what Jesus did to my grandmother and Vicki's parents. After my wife and I came to faith in 1997, we realized that our families were not Christ-followers. My grandmother was a practicing Jehovah's Witness for a while (until she got kicked out for smoking and cursing), but she held to many of their teachings. As I became a follower of Jesus, we had hard conversations. She was steeped in religion. I was steeped in grace. And grace won.

She lived with so much guilt and shame, she would often say, "I've done too much for Jehovah [God] to love me." And I would say, "God's love for you and His acceptance of you are based entirely on His Son and what He accomplished through His perfect life for you, His death on the cross for you, and His resurrection for you. Granny, it's a free gift."

What got her, though, is when I said, "Let's pray through Galatians 3:24," which says, "The law was our guardian until Christ came, in order that we might be justified by faith."

In the midst of a very hard conversation, I told my granny, "Everything you have ever done has been nailed to the cross, and all of Jesus' righteousness has been nailed to you." Over the months and years, the truth of grace not only saved her from the penalty of sin but also saved her from the power of the sin of racism. Gradually Jesus transformed the filters through which she saw Vicki. And as my grandmother lay dying in hospice care, she told me, "Dewey, Vicki is a good woman. I'm so glad you married her. I love that girl so much." These words still make me smile.

On a family vacation in Orlando in 2001 with Vicki's parents, Vicki sensed an overwhelming burden to talk to her stepfather about Jesus. At that time in his life, he had suffered two heart attacks and two bouts with cancer. His health was declining rapidly. She was not sure how much time he had left.

I love the way my father-in-law tells the story. He says, "Dewey and Vicki looked at me and Nancy [Vicki's mom] in our room. Vicki moved her chair close to mine and started crying. She then asked me, 'Do you know Jesus?'"

This conversation, in conjunction with the work God was already doing in their lives, has led to amazing things. Vicki's parents are now leaders at their church in Victor, Montana. They've led several small group studies using my first book, *Hero: Unleashing God's Power in a Man's Heart*. My father-in-law, Dick, now sees me through Jesus' filters of love. My father-in-law not only loves me, he literally dotes on me! I am the apple of his eye.

Over time, the true grace of Jesus saved him not only from the penalty of sin but also from the power of the sin of racism. Several years ago at a family reunion, he pulled me aside and said, "Dewey, I'm sorry for the way I treated you. I was wrong. You are a great man, a wonderful husband to my daughter, and a great dad. I love you. I'm so proud of you. I consider it an honor to call you son."

God's grace doesn't just save us *from* something, but *to* something: good works. "For we are God's masterpiece. He has created us anew in Christ Jesus, so we can do the good things he planned for us long ago" (Eph. 2:10 NLT).

Key 3: Know That You Have Future Grace

Now say this with me: *"I will be saved from the presence of sin"* (glorification).

I love my granny, and I had to watch her die a death no one should have had to die. Granny was more than a grandmother to me. She was my protector and my provider. I really loved her. Throughout my college years far away from home, we talked on the phone every day.

And during the years I played professional football far from home, we talked every day. I miss those conversations a lot.

My granny and I had a special bond.

When she was diagnosed with kidney cancer, her once statuesque frame was diminished in a horrifying way. I wanted so badly to help her, but I couldn't. The best I could do was to be with her as she slowly and painfully died. As I spent time with her and my family in hospice, I felt as if a part of me were dying along with her. If I could, I would try to write words that would paint a picture of the pain I went through, seeing her die this way, but there are none.

The only way I was able to endure that great sadness was through Jesus' great promises. Here are three great promises from God and His amazing grace that I can count on:

Jesus said to her, "I am the resurrection and the life. Whoever believes in me, though he die, yet shall he live, and everyone who lives and believes in me shall never die." (John 11:25–26)

"Let not your hearts be troubled. Believe in God; believe also in me. In my Father's house are many rooms. If it were not so, would I have told you that I go to prepare a place for you? And if I go and prepare a place for you, I will come again and will take you to myself, that where I am you may be also. And you know the way to where I am going." (John 14:1–4)

Then I saw a new heaven and a new earth, for the first heaven and the first earth had passed away, and the sea was no more. And I saw the holy city, New Jerusalem, coming down out of heaven from God, prepared as a bride adorned for her husband. And I heard a loud voice from the throne saying, "Behold, the dwelling place of God is with man. He will dwell with them, and they will be his people, and God himself will be with them as their God. He will wipe away every tear from their eyes, and death shall be no more, neither shall there be mourning, nor crying, nor pain anymore, for the former things have passed away." And he who was seated on the throne said, "Behold, I am making all things new." (Rev. 21:1–5)

As I was leaving my granny's hospice room to head to the airport, she lifted up her head and said, unexpectedly, because she had been so incoherent for days, "Dewey, you are a wonderful father and husband. You are a great man. I'm so proud of you." Then she lay back down. Several weeks later, I preached her funeral.

I shed tears. But the tears I shed were not tears of sadness or hopelessness. They were tears of joy and hope. Because of Jesus' promises, I knew I would not only hear her voice again, but I would see her again with a new, glorified, resurrected body in the new heaven and new earth, a sin-free environment.

C. S. Lewis expressed my own heart when he wrote, "It was only the beginning of the real story. All their life in this world . . . had only been the cover and the title page; now at least they were beginning Chapter One of the Great Story, which no one on the earth has read, which goes on forever and in which every chapter is better than the one before."[1]

We have been saved from the penalty of sin; Jesus is our righteousness. We are being saved from the power of sin; Jesus is our sanctification. And we will be saved from the presence of sin; Jesus is our hope for future glorification in the new heaven and earth.[2] This is the gospel of grace.

TRANSFORMATION MOMENT

Head

GRACE is *God's Righteousness At Christ's Expense*. God the Father has declared you to be the very righteousness of Jesus based completely on the finished work of Jesus. You are accepted, loved, and blessed because you are "in" Christ. All of your unrighteousness was nailed to Jesus on the cross, and all His righteousness was nailed to you when you trusted Him as your Savior God and King.

Heart

Pray:

Papa, it amazes me that grace is truly this amazing. I find it hard to believe that You accept, love, and bless me based on the work and accomplishments of another, Jesus. Give me the grace to believe I am in Christ and that Christ is in me. In Jesus' name, amen.

Hands

Write out this chart[3] every day for a week and share it with someone:

	RELIGION	GRACE
Says	"Do"	"Done"
Emphasis	What we do	What God does
Lives out of	The flesh (self-life)	The Holy Spirit (Christ-life)
Draws on	Our resources	God's resources

	RELIGION	**GRACE**
Deals with	External rules, regulations	Inner heart attitude
Primary focus	Ought to, should, must	Want to
Creates	Bondage, duty, obligation	Freedom
Lives life from the	Outside in	Inside out
Declares	"Do in order to be"	"You are; therefore you do"
Produces	Guilt and condemnation	Acceptance and security
Leads to	Defeat	Victory

SEVEN

FROM CONSUMER TO CONTRIBUTOR

The world is not interested in what we do for a living. What they are interested in is what we have to offer freely—hope, strength, love and the power to make a difference!

—Sasha Azevedo

IF YOU AND I WERE TO RECORD OUR PRAYERS, WHAT WOULD THEY sound like? Would they be an ongoing monologue of us asking God for things? Would we sound like a seven-year-old in Target who begs for a different toy in each aisle? If we actually heard ourselves pray, would it be a long list of "God give me" over and over? *And are the things we request from God going to help us become more like Jesus and advance*

His kingdom, or are they just to satisfy us and make us more comfortable in this life?

What if all your children did was ask you for things? What if everything was about what they wanted and what they thought they just couldn't live without? After a while, you would start to feel as though they believed your sole reason for existing was to give them what they want when they want it. You'd start to feel like a prostitute. You would begin to feel used by your children, not loved by them.

I wonder if God feels this way when all we do is approach Him as if He were some kind of ATM in the sky? Sadly, many people find themselves disappointed in a false version of Christianity because Jesus said, "Ask and you shall receive." They asked Jesus, but they did not receive what they wanted, so now they are disillusioned and angry.

Here's the deal: Jesus will gladly give us what we ask for when what we request of Him advances His kingdom on earth by bringing His Father glory. Jesus delights in answering prayers that reflect His words: "Your [God's] kingdom come, your will be done, on earth as it is in heaven" (Matt. 6:9). He said, "But if you remain in me and my words remain in you, you may ask for anything you want, and it will be granted! When you produce much fruit, you are my true disciples. This brings great glory to my Father" (John 15:7–8 NLT).

You see, we exist for God. God does not exist for us. He doesn't orbit around us as though we are the center of the universe. We orbit around Him and His purposes.

THE EMPTY SELF OF THE CONSUMER

I pray that as you read this book, you will sense deep in your heart that I love you and desire the best for you. I want to see you be and do all that King Jesus has intended for you. But my primary motivation is that you would see that it is for Jesus and His glory, not yours. "Not to us, O Lord, not to us, but to your name goes all the glory for your unfailing love and faithfulness," says Psalm 115:1 (NLT). When we are about Jesus' glory, we will be about doing what's best for people.

Consumerism is an enemy that acts like acid. It eats away at everything it touches. Consumerism is fueled by an epidemic in America called "the Empty Self," a term coined by psychologist Philip Cushman, PhD, of the California School of Professional Psychology.[1] Our tendency for excessive consumption is fed by a void we feel, a hole that we are trying desperately to fill with stuff. Let me share with you four characteristics of "the Empty Self" from J. P. Moreland's *Kingdom Triangle*.[2]

The Empty Self Is Very Individualistic

The empty self is all about itself. Its hopes and dreams revolve around making its life better and more comfortable at others' expense. It has very little concern for the needs of those around it unless meeting someone else's needs helps it achieve its desires.

For example, people with the empty self will choose a church to "go to" if the sermons are good and make them feel better and if the music is their kind of music. The empty self is not concerned about the church's vision or how he or she can make that vision grow and have an impact in the world. What matters is that the church meets that individual's needs. And once it doesn't anymore, the empty self will go in search of one that does.

The Empty Self Is Infantile

The empty self seeks to be made happy by food, entertainment, and other consumer goods. It must have its desires satisfied immediately; delayed gratification is seen as repulsive. It has to be pacified because it can't handle when desires aren't met instantly. It's preoccupied with sex, physical appearance, body image, and the need to feel good all the time. Boredom is a supreme evil, and amusement is heaven.

The Empty Self Is Narcissistic

Narcissism is an over-the-top sense of what I call a "self-crush," in which the individual is obsessed by, and only by, his or her own self-interest and personal fulfillment. Narcissists manipulate people and try to manipulate God to validate their own needs for power and the admiration of others. God and the people around him or her are the narcissist's servants for meeting his or her own needs.

The Empty Self Is Passive

People with the empty self are fixed on living their lives through the risks, challenges, and adventures of others. Perhaps this is why reality shows have taken off in popularity in recent years. The empty self is passive in the sense that he or she would rather do nothing and let life zip right by than to actually participate in life in a meaningful way. His or her primary purpose is to be entertained with as little energy expended as possible. Simply put, empty selves are in search of pleasure provided by others.

The gospel truth is that the empty self is a label that Jesus will gladly strip away in order to give you a new label and a new life: "All of God lives fully in Christ (even when Christ was on earth), and you have a full and true life in Christ, who is ruler over all rulers and powers" (Col. 2:9–10 NCV). This full and true life we receive from Jesus will change you from consumer to contributor.

Consumers are empty selves. Contributors are maturing in their "full and true life in Christ." Consumers live limited lives. Contributors live without limits because they are participating in the "full and true life in Christ." Contributors are ambassadors in God's kingdom.

When you signed up to follow Jesus, He branded your soul with a new label: "Contributor." This is who you are in Christ. This is your new identity. It's now time to walk in your divine birthright.

THE CHILDISHNESS OF THE CONSUMER

The nature of the relationship Vicki and I have with our children has changed as they have matured. When my children were little, they saw my wife and me as their providers. When they were babies, all they did was consume. And never once was there a "You know, Mom and Dad, I want to thank you for providing for my every need. I love you so much. In response to your great love and care for me, how might I serve you and add to this family's well-being?"

As babies, my kids did not have the capacity to be grateful or the ability to contribute to the Gray family. But as they have matured, they love us for us, not simply for what we give them. And they add value to the family by contributing. Our children moved from being consumers to being contributors. Jesus wants us to move from consumers to contributors too. Becoming a contributor to God's kingdom unleashes a limitless life for the glory of God.

Infants Consume—Adults Contribute

The reason we approach God as if He's Santa Claus is because we have embraced a worldview called *consumerism*.

Consumerism places the consumer at the center of the universe and affirms that the goal of life is to satisfy one's unmet desires and avoid discomfort by consuming goods, experiences, and other people.[3]

Consider this for a moment: every commercial on television is trying to create a need in our lives for that product to satisfy. By buying and consuming the product, our lives will become better and more comfortable. The marketer's job is to place you and me at the center of the universe so they can sell their expensive products to us to meet our supposed needs, which they created. Unfortunately, we take this very same consumerist worldview to Jesus and His Church.

Jesus, You died for me! Yes, that is gloriously true. But why did He die for you? Was it to build your kingdom on earth, or His?

Jesus can and does provide for us! That, too, is gloriously true. But why does He provide for us? Is it so we can escape pain and discomfort, or is it to display His glory by being generous to others in need?

Jesus has created the Church for us! And yes, that is also gloriously true. But why did He create the Church? Is it a place we go to simply have our needs met, or is the Church people on a mission to continue Jesus' ministry? Even as pastors we can be tempted to try to outmarket one another so we can attract consumers (I mean, people) to our church. We try to have the nicest, newest church building because the church down the street has a cutting-edge building with an amazing Disneyland-like children's ministry wing. We have to keep up with our competition or our people will go there.

We have to make sure we have the latest technology in our church building because the new church down the street is drawing all the consumers (I mean, people) to its Sunday show (uh, worship experience). We have to step up our game, too, so we don't get left behind.

Okay. You get the point.

Having a nice worship facility is important. At Transformation Church, we have transformed an old warehouse into a wonderful facility to equip and train missionaries—that's what I call our congregation. And we have technology to communicate the unchanging truth in a relevant way so people in the twenty-first century can understand the gospel.

Our facility fits our vision and values. We will be excellent without being extravagant. I'm just trying to make a point that even we pastors turn into marketers and turn people who are made in the image of God into consumers. This is dehumanizing and debilitating to Jesus' bride, His Church.

Pastors, in the long run this hurts the church deeply because it produces consumers instead of contributors. Our competition is not the other local churches or the mall or the movies. In fact, we are not competing against any "flesh-and-blood enemies, but against evil rulers and authorities of the unseen world, against mighty powers in this dark world, and against evil spirits in the heavenly places" (Eph. 6:12 NLT).

Pastors, we must not let consumerism drive our philosophy of ministry. Consumerism is limiting.

GROWING PAST CONSUMERISM

Jesus' Jewish disciples asked Him to teach them to pray. So Jesus said, "When you pray, gentlemen, this is how you should do it." And he prayed:

> Our Father in heaven, hallowed be your name. Your kingdom come, your will be done, on earth as it is in heaven.

Give us this day our daily bread, and forgive us our debts,
as we also have forgiven our debtors. And lead us not into
temptation, but deliver us from evil. (Matt. 6:9–13)

Consumerism says that because I've trusted Jesus, He has
given me every spiritual blessing in Christ so that I will escape
hell. He will also give me love, peace, power, and the stuff I
need so I can realize my potential and fulfill my dreams on
earth. Now, most people I know in the Christian community
would not say those exact words, but when you sit down with
them and get below the surface, a consumerist worldview is
alive and well.

A contributor says that because I've trusted Jesus, God
has given me every spiritual blessing in Christ so that His
kingdom will come to earth through my life. Jesus' love,
grace, power, and provision are given so that His rule and
reign will be established on earth as it is heaven, through His
church.

All of us start our journey with Jesus as consumers. We
begin a marriage journey the same way. When I married my
wife twenty-one years ago, I loved her for much different reasons
than I love her now. Early in our marriage, I was a consumer. It
was about what I could get from her. Now, as her sacrificial love
and unwavering respect have waged war on my selfish heart, I
love her for her, and I want to add value to her life.

Jesus wants us to grow from being consumers to become
contributors. When He taught His early disciples to pray,
He was teaching them how to move from being consumers to becoming contributors to His kingdom. Let's spend a
moment in the Lord's Prayer, which really could be called the
"Disciples' Prayer."

Becoming Abba's Child

"Our Father in heaven . . ."

Jesus rocked His disciples' world by teaching them to address YHWH (God) as Abba. *Abba* is an Aramaic term that would be equivalent to the English word *daddy* or *papa.*

At Transformation Church, little children will run toward me with their arms raised high in the air, wanting me to pick them up. And, of course, I do. The word *Abba* expresses a Father who longs for His children to run toward Him, arms raised high, so He can lift them up. When we pray, we are praying to the King of the universe, who has all power, all honor, and all glory! Yet He hungers for His children to call Him Papa so He can lift us up and put us on His lap.

Honoring His Name, Not Our Desires

". . . hallowed be your name."

We do not use the word *hallowed* very much, if ever, but it expresses honor, reverence, and respect. To "hallow" is to be in awe of someone great. Perhaps this illustration will help convey its meaning.

My former high school coach, D. W. Rutledge, is a man of mountain-size integrity. I respect him immensely. My senior year in high school, I was selected to play in the 1989 Whataburger Texas High School Football All-Star game. I rode five hours, from San Antonio to Dallas, with Coach Rutledge. I said about five words that entire trip. The reason I was so quiet is because I was in awe of him. Even to this day when I'm around him, I call him Coach Rutledge. I honor him.

How much more should we honor God the Papa? This is what the word *hallowed* is communicating to us. To honor God the Father is to be perpetually aware that in every moment, in every thought, and in every action, we are to acknowledge and to be in awe of the God who is always present with us. When we are in God's presence, there is no such thing as secular and sacred. All of life is sacred because we are honoring God the Papa in the everydayness of life.

Seeking His Kingdom, Not Our Own

"Your kingdom come, your will be done, on earth as it is in heaven."

From all eternity, God has had a dream to establish His kingdom on earth as it is in heaven. Ephesians 3:10–11 describes it this way: *"so that through the church* the manifold wisdom of God might now be made known to the rulers and authorities in the heavenly places. This was according to the *eternal purpose* that he has realized in Christ Jesus our Lord" (emphasis added).

God the Papa's eternal purpose is to establish His kingdom on earth through His people, the Church. God began carrying out His eternal purpose with Adam, then Israel, then Jesus. He is fulfilling it now through Jesus' bride, the Church. So when Jesus came to earth, it was an invasion of sorts. God was establishing His kingdom. Everything Jesus did for thirty-three years—His miracles, His teachings, His sinless life, His atoning death, resurrection, and ascension to the right hand of His Father—was Him saying, "The kingdom of God has arrived."

And now, the Church has everything she needs to continue Jesus' mission and fulfill His Father's eternal purpose. "His divine power has granted to us all things that pertain to life and godliness, through the knowledge of him who called us to his own glory and excellence" (2 Peter 1:3).

You see, Jesus rescued us and gave us a new identity—His Church. And with this new identity, He provides everything we need for life and to help us achieve godliness for Jesus' own glory and excellence.

Jesus Is Our Daily Bread

"Give us this day our daily bread . . ."

When God's people, the Israelites, were wandering in the desert after they'd been rescued from slavery in Egypt, God caused manna, or what I call *soul-food* from heaven, to fall down upon them so they could eat and live. When Jesus told His disciples to pray for God to provide daily bread, they would have known this story. Jesus would later reveal to His disciples that He is the Bread of Life.

So when we ask God to give us our daily bread, we are affirming that Jesus is our source for physical, spiritual, and emotional substance. He is our soul-food. He is the Great Provider of all that we need. We are to long for Jesus as we long for our next meal. Jesus provides our needs so we can be equipped to advance His Daddy's kingdom.

Forgiven People Forgive

". . . and forgive us our debts, as we also have forgiven our debtors."

As the lead pastor of Transformation Church, I smell like the sheep of Transformation Church. This means I counsel people throughout the week, and the scent of their pain, problems, and past wounds accompanies me. One of the things that shocks me is how married Christians who claim to be freely forgiven by Jesus refuse to forgive each other, even though the Bible says to "be kind to each other, tenderhearted, forgiving one another, just as God through Christ has forgiven you" (Eph. 4:32 NLT).

When we calculate the debt that Jesus forgives us for, we

will find it easier, although not easy, to give the same forgiveness we've experienced to one another. Forgiven people forgive others.

Winning

"And lead us not into temptation, but deliver us from evil."

When I played high school football at Converse Judson, oftentimes we won the game before we even played it. Our opponents were intimated by our passion, execution, and relentless team play. They knew we were going to win even before we played. And we did.

Because we are on "Team Jesus," we, too, have already won the game of life. We live from Jesus' victory over sin, death, and evil.

In the Disciples' Prayer, we see that God has established His kingdom on earth through His Church, and He has provided all that we need to advance His kingdom. Jesus is interested in creating contributors, not consumers.

TIME FOR A NEW LABEL . . . "CONTRIBUTOR"

Our identity in Christ is so much broader, deeper, and richer than we often realize and experience. We are so intertwined with Jesus that even our citizenship has been made new through our eternal association with Him as His beautiful bride, the Church.

Here are the keys to becoming a contributing bride rather than a consuming one:

Key 1: Know That You Are an Ambassador

An ambassador is an authorized messenger or representative of a higher authority. The Higher Authority we represent is the King of kings, Jesus. Jesus' interests have now become our interests. His passions have become our passions. His mission has become our mission. Why? Because we are His ambassadors on earth.

As His ambassadors, we have been sent on a mission into a foreign land to speak and act on behalf of our King. Perhaps you're saying, "Pastor Derwin, I'm not in a foreign land." Yes, you are. The gospel truth is this: Christ, our true King, hails from a different realm. He returned to earth to rightly claim what is His. And because we are "in" Christ our King, we, too, are now from a different realm and have a different citizenship. This realm is called heaven, the very realm of God: *"But our citizenship is in heaven, and from it we await a Savior, the Lord Jesus Christ, who will transform our lowly body to be like his glorious body, by the power that enables him even to subject all things to himself"* (Phil. 3:20–21, emphasis added).

When you and I wake up in the morning as Jesus' ambassadors, instead of looking for ways to get comfortable in this world, we look for ways to *re*-present our King to our fractured world—riddled with injustice, violence, and poverty—and to transform it as a sign that the King is back. Every morning is new, filled with divine possibilities.

The kingdom of God is at hand! Jesus is occupying and colonizing earth with a people He calls His body, who are controlled by His love, which compels them to enter into and promote His mission on earth. "Now you are the body of Christ and individually members of it" (1 Cor. 12:27).

Key 2: Know That Christ's Ambassadors Are Controlled by His Love

I love Jesus because He first loved me. From the very moment Jesus pulverized my heart with His grace, I have been in love with Him. I did not even know what love was until Jesus first loved me.

Early in my faith, in 2001, I happened upon a book entitled *Face to Face* by Dr. Ken Boa. I resonated with Boa's writings because he is a first-rate scholar, but his heart beats Jesus' gospel of grace. He understood that the Church exists on earth to reveal the kingdom of God. As I read the words I'm about to share with you, the trajectory of my life and Transformation Church began to be formed,

> *Loving God completely* [upward] is a growth process that involves the personal elements of communication and response. By listening to the Holy Spirit in the words of Scripture and speaking to the Lord in our thoughts and prayers, we move in the direction of knowing Him better. The better we know Him, the more we will love Him, and the more we love Him, the greater will be our willingness to respond to Him in trust and obedience.
>
> To *love ourselves correctly* [inward] is to see ourselves as God sees us and to allow the Word, not the world, to define who and whose we really are. The clearer we capture the vision of our new identity in Jesus Christ, the more we will realize that our deepest needs for security, significance and satisfaction are met in Him and not in people, possessions or positions.
>
> A Biblical view of our identity and resources in Christ moves us in the direction of *loving others compassionately* [outward]. Grasping our true and unlimited resources in Christ frees us from bondage to the opinions of others and gives us the liberty to love and serve others regardless of their response.[4]

Boa was simply communicating Jesus' words from the Hebrew Shema, which, as quoted in Matthew, says, "You shall love the Lord your God with all your heart and with all your soul and with all your mind. This is the great and first commandment. And a second is like it: You shall love your neighbor as yourself. On these two commandments depend all the Law and the Prophets" (22:37–39).

The Hebrew word *shema* means "to listen with the heart and obey." In essence, Jesus, God incarnate, was saying that the entire Bible, from the Law to the Prophets, is a story about Him, as we see in John 5:39: "You search the scriptures because you think they give you eternal life. But the scriptures point to me!" (NLT). Jesus is the glory of God, and God's glory is revealed through a redeemed people who love God and love their neighbors the way they love themselves. This is the kingdom of God.

In his book *Face to Face*, Boa developed a concise and very effective way to say this: "Upward—Love God completely. Inward—Love yourself correctly. Outward—Love your neighbor compassionately. Upward, Inward, Outward is my life's vision statement."

And it's a part of the vision of Transformation Church. Our vision is to be "a multi-ethnic, multi-generational, mission-shaped community that loves God completely (Upward), ourselves correctly (Inward), and our neighbors compassionately (Outward)."[5]

Upward, Inward, Outward is God's blueprint for humanity. We become more human when we allow the Spirit to progressively, moment by moment, transform us into Upward, Inward, Outward people. This is God's goal for our lives. Upward, Inward, Outward people are His ambassadors who spread Jesus' kingdom on earth.

I'm often asked, "How has Transformation Church grown so fast?" I'll say, "The favor of God is upon us. We are in a tsunami of His grace. And I think we've grown because of our Upward, Inward, Outward vision. For us, discipleship and evangelism are two sides of the same coin. The same gospel that introduces people to Jesus propels them to grow in Jesus."

Ambassadors of Jesus represent the King because they love the King in response to the King loving them with His steadfast love. The apostle Paul says it this way:

For the love of Christ controls us. (2 Cor. 5:14)

We are ruled by the love of Christ. (2 Cor. 5:14 GNT)

Christ's love has moved me to such extremes. His love has the first and last word in everything we do. (2 Cor. 5:14 MSG)

I love how the various translations communicate what Jesus' love does in the lives of His ambassadors: "controls" us; "rules" us; "moves" us. An ambassador is controlled, ruled, and moved by the love of Jesus to live a Spirit-empowered life for the glory of God. His mission becomes our mission. What breaks His heart begins to break ours.

Together, let's *shema*, or listen with our whole hearts, to the full weight of this glorious text: "For the love of Christ controls us, because we have concluded this: that one has died for all, therefore all have died; and he died for all, that those who live might no longer live for themselves but for him who for their sake died and was raised" (2 Cor. 5:14–15).

Key 3: Know That an Ambassador Lives for the Glory of Another

An ambassador of Christ lives for the glory of Another, the resurrected King. Jesus' resurrection was a sign to the world that God's kingdom had indeed come to earth and that one day not only His followers would be resurrected, but the entire universe would be also. All things will be made new. Ambassadors "no longer live for themselves but for him who for their sake died and was raised" (2 Cor. 5:15).

Wow. If there was ever a statement that drop-kicked consumerism in the teeth, this is it. Our time, talents, and treasure are on loan to us from God. He graciously gave them to us so we could join Him in advancing His kingdom on earth. Think about it:

Do we really think God gave us the abilities we have just for our own glory?

Do we think God has given us the jobs we have simply so we can make money, pay off debt, and buy more stuff?

As ambassadors of Jesus, we see the entirety of our lives as His platform in which His kingdom is spread to every corner of this planet. We see our schools as our mission field.

We see our jobs as our mission field. We even see the money we have as His money to advance His kingdom.

How We Spend Money Reflects What We Truly Value

If you want to know what a person believes about Jesus, ask if you can see how he spends his money. For where your heart is, your money will be also. I'm thoroughly convinced one of the areas of discipleship the church overlooks is the correlation between how we use money and our spiritual maturity. The more generous we realize Jesus was to us, the more generous we become with our money in the local church.

There are two thousand verses in the Bible—including

sixteen of Jesus' thirty-eight parables—about money and possessions. And there are three times as many verses on money in the Bible as on love.

Put Your Money Where Your Heart Is

While sitting in a New Testament class several years ago, my heart started pounding as we studied Ephesians 4:11–16. This text says God gave gifts to His Church. These gifts are people who are to lead His Church. Their role is to equip God's people for the work of ministry so His Church will be built up in love. My soul was arrested.

I knew God was calling me to shepherd a community of faith back in 2004. I fought the calling for several years, but eventually God led me on a journey that brought me to plant Transformation Church. My wife, Vicki, and I and one of her best friends, Angela, were the church-planting team. Vicki and I turned our dining room into an office. For weeks we crafted what would be the vision and values of Transformation Church. On a piece of white paper, Transformation Church looked great! One huge problem, though: we did not have enough "green" paper (money) to launch this great church.

I'm stingy by nature. I grew up poor. And when I played in the NFL, I wanted to keep my money! Sure, I helped my family in Texas, and I had a foundation that did charitable giving. But trust me, I was stingy. So when Jesus invaded my life, one of the last areas I turned over to Him was my money. For the first six to eight months of following Jesus, I did not give anything at offering time in church.

But the more Jesus gripped my heart, the more my life was transformed. The things that mattered to Him began to matter to me. People matter to Jesus; therefore my wife and I started giving generously to the local church where we were

members, so people could come to faith and experience Jesus'
amazing grace.

THE GOD WITHOUT LIMITS

Contributions from Unexpected Places

As we were trying to raise money to launch Transformation
Church in the summer and fall of 2009, we sensed God saying, *If
you want Transformation Church to be generous, you need to show
them how to be by setting an example.* So we had a family meeting in the fall 2009. My son, Jeremiah, was oblivious to money,
but my daughter, Presley, who was thirteen at the time, was
not. I shared with them how we as a family would sacrificially
give money to start Transformation Church because we believed
Jesus would transform the world through it.

Presley said, "Dad, if we give this much money, how am I
going to get a car in a few years?"

"I don't know, honey, but we're going to trust Jesus to provide for us."

I knew that if the dream on paper called Transformation
Church was to live, then I needed an experienced executive pas-
tor. Through a set of amazing circumstances, God brought Pastor
Paul Allen into my life, and our vision resonated with him.

One day we sat on a curb outside a potential building space,
and I said, "Paul, I believe God is going to transform the world
through Transformation Church. In thirty years, people will say
God used Transformation Church to change the landscape of
Christianity in America. Because of them and others, multiethnic
congregations on a mission will be the norm in America."

Then I said, "I'm supposed to make $68,000 this year. But
that money does not exist. I believe so much in what Jesus is going

to do that I'm willing to split my imaginary salary of $68,000 with you. We will start with an imaginary $34,000 each. Are you in?"

And he said, "Yes, I'm in."

Does the way you spend the money God has given you the ability to earn reflect that you honor His kingdom, or yours? For some of you, giving God 10 percent is a tip. It doesn't alter your lifestyle at all.

The reason my wife and I give generously to our local church, and the reason I want you to start giving as well, is because people matter to Jesus. Would you *listen with your whole heart* (*shema*) to the text below? You'll be blessed by it.

Remember this—a farmer who plants only a few seeds will get a small crop. But the one who plants generously will get a generous crop. You must each decide in your heart how much to give. And don't give reluctantly or in response to pressure. "For God loves a person who gives cheerfully." And God will generously provide all you need. Then you will always have everything you need and plenty left over to share with others. . . . For God is the One who provides seed for the farmer and then bread to eat. In the same way, He will provide and increase your resources and then produce a great harvest of generosity in you. Yes, you will be enriched in every way so that you can always be generous. And when we take your gifts to those who need them, they will thank God. So two good things will result from this ministry of giving—the needs of the believers in Jerusalem will be met, and they will joyfully express their thanks to God. As a result of your ministry, they will give glory to God. For your generosity to them and to all believers will prove that you are obedient to the Good News of Christ. And they will pray

> for you with deep affection because of the overflowing grace
> God has given to you. Thank God for this gift too wonderful for
> words! (2 Cor. 9:6–8, 10–15 NLT)

My family and I gave "gulp" financial gifts when we started Transformation Church. A gulp gift is when you write a check or cash in a mutual fund, and when you look at the amount, it makes you gulp. We gave a gulp gift when Transformation Church needed to expand into the next warehouse bay because we were growing so fast. We gave another gulp gift when Transformation Church started our first multisite campus in Rock Hill, South Carolina.

And you know what? I would never go back to life the way it was before planting Transformation Church. The more financially generous we've become, the more God has shown up in miraculous ways, and the greater our faith and our love for Him and His Bride, the Church, has grown.

And God has provided for our every need. Oh yeah, and my wife and I were able to buy my daughter, Presley, a car on her sixteenth birthday. You can't outgive God.

MARINATE ON THAT!

We often fail to see God do epic things in our lives because we do not position ourselves in such a way for Him to show up and show off. We trust our savings instead of Jesus. We give God a "tip" on Sundays instead of giving generously. We sin in this way because consumerism has us in a "heart-lock." As Jesus grabs our hearts with His grace, we begin to see people through His eyes.

As God unlocks generosity in hearts and defeats consumerism, let's now move to another key so God can fling open our hearts to all that He has for us.

Key 4: Know That Ambassadors Are Reconcilers

Ambassadors of Jesus are passionate about reconciling people who are far from Christ back to Him. Do you wake in the morning with a sense of urgency? I hope you do. The stakes are high. Look at Romans 5:10–11: "For if while we were enemies we were reconciled to God by the death of his Son, much more, now that we are reconciled, shall we be saved by his life. More than that, we also rejoice in God through our Lord Jesus Christ, through whom we have now received reconciliation."

Outside of association and allegiance to Jesus, humanity is God's enemy. Reread Romans 5:10–11 in the previous paragraph. This is why ambassadors of Jesus awake in the morning with a sense of urgency. They feel deeply that their time, talents, and treasure are to be leveraged so that God's enemies can be reconciled to God through Jesus. As we learned earlier, reconciliation means that through Jesus' life, death, resurrection, and exaltation, God's enemies become His friends.

When you signed up to follow Jesus, He gave you the ministry of reconciliation. You are a reconciler. Your life is a bridge over which people walk from death to life.

> All this is from God, who through Christ reconciled us to himself and gave us the ministry of reconciliation; that is, in Christ, God was reconciling the world to himself, not counting their trespasses against them, and entrusting to us the message of reconciliation. Therefore, we are ambassadors for Christ, God making his appeal through us. We implore you on behalf of Christ, be reconciled to

God. For our sake he made him to be sin who knew no sin, so that in him we might become the righteousness of God. (2 Cor. 5:18–21)

There are people in your sphere of influence who live under the crushing weight of sin, shame, and guilt, and worst of all, they are God's enemies. But God has entrusted you and me, His Church, with the message of reconciliation. Are you giving that message away?

God *pleads* with people to become His friends through our lives. A hurting world needs to know that Jesus became what God hates most—sin—so that they could become what He loves most: His children.

For all eternity, followers of Jesus will enjoy Jesus and one another. But we will not share the message of reconciliation. There will be no need to. But there is a need now! That's why Jesus left us here as His ambassadors to announce that the kingdom of God has come and that salvation belongs to our God. You are not a consumer. You are a contributor, an ambassador of Christ. And you are limitless in Christ.

TRANSFORMATION MOMENT

Head

You are an ambassador of Christ. You are in a foreign land, announcing through your life and words that the kingdom of God has come. Your time, talents, and treasure are now a platform on which Jesus can rule and reign.

Heart

Pray:

Papa, Your kingdom has come. Everything Jesus said and did was an announcement that Your kingdom has arrived on earth. And now, through my association with Him, I am His ambassador. My time, my talents, and my treasure are gifts from You to be leveraged for Your kingdom. You have graciously reconciled me to You so I now can be a reconciler. I refuse, by the indwelling of Christ, to let consumerism rob me of my great adventure with You. Thank You, Lord God, for making me Your ambassador. In Jesus' name, amen.

Hands

- Think about ways consumerism has influenced your life. Repent, and move from being a consumer to being a contributor.
- Develop a financial budget and start giving sacrificially, generously, and consistently to your local church.
- Start serving in your local church.
- Begin sharing the message of reconciliation with people in your sphere of influence who do not know Christ.

EIGHT

FROM PURPOSELESS TO PURPOSEFUL

*The purpose of your life is far greater than your own
personal fulfillment, your peace of mind, or even
your happiness. It's far greater than your family, your
career, or even your wildest dreams and ambitions.
If you want to know why you were placed on this
planet, you must begin with God. You were born by his
purpose and for his purpose.*

—**Rick Warren,** *The Purpose Driven Life*

"WHAT'S GOD'S WILL FOR MY LIFE?"

If I had a five-dollar bill for every time I've been asked
that question, I would be a very wealthy man. The frequency
with which this question comes up gives insight into just how

important it is to humanity. People want to know why they are here at this time in history and what they are supposed to do with their lives.

When I was in my late twenties, that question, among others, haunted me like a bad dream. *What will I do after my NFL career is over? Will what I do provide for my young family? Will I be good at what I do? Will my post-NFL career bring me joy? Will what I do really matter and make a difference?*

My wife and I recently met with a freshly retired NFL player and his wife who are members of Transformation Church. This is a very difficult time for former NFL players. It's a time of soul-searching. He asked the same exact questions I asked when I was transitioning from the NFL to the next chapter of my life. We all want to know our purpose.

Perhaps you are asking these very questions about your purpose right now. Our sacred vocations (jobs), through which Jesus expresses Himself through us in the workplace, are not our purpose; they are conduits of how our purpose is expressed. (We'll examine this more in chapter 9.)

The first and most important question each of us needs to answer is: "Who am I to be in the world?" Another way of saying that is, "What self-identity will determine my function?" A person's identity determines his or her function in life. Unfortunately, the great majority of people focus on their function instead of their identity. Thus, a lot of people are functioning in life in areas where they do not have ultimate joy because they are trying to establish who they are on what they do. When you know your identity, discovering your function in life follows.

Your identity must be built on something solid, immovable, and unchanging. Finding your purpose in what you *do* is like building your house in sand. When the Hurricane Katrinas of life blow your way, a house built on sand will be destroyed because its foundation is unreliable.

Who you are is vastly more important than what you do. And when you know who you are, you will be able to know what you are supposed do. If you and I do not allow God to develop our identities, we will try to discover them through possessions, people, and popularity. This is like putting an expensive suit on a dead man. It's a funeral.

Millions of people exist in a living funeral because they've neglected to discover their identities. They have their "dream jobs," or they are married to the spouses of their fantasies; yet joy evades them. We say to ourselves:

"If I could just make more money, I'd really be happy."
"If I left my wife for her, I'd really be happy."
"If I can just get that promotion, I'd really be happy."

Before we know it, we've lived a life of "If I could only ____, then I'd be happy," and ultimately we never find joy.

MOVING BEYOND PURPOSELESS: LET JESUS SHAPE YOUR IDENTITY

When our identity and character are shaped by Jesus, His thoughts, His character, and His actions become ours.

When I think of loving my wife, children, and the Transformation Church family with Jesus' thoughts, character, and actions, then the circuits in my heart explode with, *Yes, I want that!* That is limitless life! Let these identity-defining words forge your heart to reflect the heart of the One who created you for Himself:

The Mind of Christ

"Do nothing from selfish ambition or conceit, but in humility count others more significant than yourselves. Let each of you look not only to his own interests, but also to the interests of others. Have this mind among yourselves, which is yours in Christ Jesus" (Phil. 2:3–5).

The Character of Christ

"Since God chose you to be the holy people he loves, you must clothe yourselves with tenderhearted mercy, kindness, humility, gentleness, and patience. Make allowance for each other's faults, and forgive anyone who offends you. Remember, the Lord forgave you, so you must forgive others. Above all, clothe yourselves with love, which binds us all together in perfect harmony. And let the peace that comes from Christ rule in your hearts. For as members of one body you are called to live in peace. And always be thankful" (Col. 3:12–15 NLT).

The Actions of Christ

"And whatever you do or say, do it as a representative of the Lord Jesus, giving thanks through him to God the Father" (Col. 3:17 NLT).

The Power of Christ

"That's why I work and struggle so hard, depending on Christ's mighty power that works within me" (Col. 1:29 NLT).

People who are shaped by Jesus live without limits. Understand, to live a limitless life does not mean you will be made famous, but it does mean that Jesus will be famous through your life. And when that happens, joy will fill your soul. You've been created to live without limits. Let's go claim our divine birthright by finding our purpose.

MOVING BEYOND PURPOSELESS: LET GOD LOVE YOU

Your purpose for existing is this: to let God the Father love you.

Does this excite you? Were you looking for something more? If you were, disappointment and disillusionment with life will cling to you like your skin.

Think about it: America is the richest country in the history of humanity, and we are still miserable. Why? Because we've found our purpose not in being loved by God the Papa, but by loving the prosperity with which God the Papa has blessed us. And that blessing is now a curse, because blessings are not designed to give us purpose. Rather, our purpose is found in the One who blessed us.

Still Haven't Found What I'm Looking For

I have lived the American Dream. I've been on TV since I was seventeen and signed autographs since I was eighteen. I've been a famous professional football player (at least according to my mom), partied with celebrities, and worked on TV. I have a wonderful woman who has dazzled me with her beauty for more than twenty years. Yet none of those external things gave me the joy that only Jesus can provide.

Joy is found in living in our purpose, and our purpose is to let God love us. Then and only then will we know our individual paths in life. David proclaimed, "You reveal the path of life to me; in Your presence is abundant joy; in Your right hand are eternal pleasures" (Ps. 16:11 HCSB).

MARINATE ON THAT!

If God created the universe, and even holds it together like cosmic glue, do you really think He created you just to *do* stuff for Him, like some kind of minion? God is more concerned with you beholding His beauty and being transformed into His image as His beauty captures your heart from the rival gods of this world. That's always been His highest desire.

The Bible says:

- "God said, 'Let us make man in our image, after our likeness'" (Gen. 1:26).
- "And we all, with unveiled face, beholding the glory of the Lord, are being transformed into the same image from one degree of glory to another" (2 Cor. 3:18).
- "Be renewed in the spirit of your minds, and . . . put on the new self, created after the likeness of God in true righteousness and holiness" (Eph. 4:23–24).

Our purpose is to simply let God love us, and as we gaze into His eyes, we are transformed into His beautiful image. A limitless life is a beautiful life that flows out of the Beautiful One.

One of the greatest compliments I've ever received was from an uncle of mine who is an atheist. After I preached my grandmother's funeral, I lined up all the men in my family, including my son, Jeremiah, and prayed a prayer of blessing over them. My atheist uncle said to me in a thoughtful voice, "Dewey, you are a beautiful man." I think that was the best way he could describe seeing Jesus in me during that time of hurt.

I share this story with you because what he said to me was an answer to prayer. With tears, I had prayed for years that my family, some of whom are far from Jesus, would see Jesus when I'm near. As we behold the Beautiful One, we become beautiful people.

The world needs more beautiful people.

Reality check: When we pray, do we ask God to make us beautiful people, transformed into His image, or do we ask Him more often about getting us the jobs we want, the spouses we want, the money we need? What if you get all those things but you are not a beautiful, Jesus-reflecting person? A limited life would be one in which we have everything, yet we are not beautiful, Jesus-reflecting people.

"Will You Let Me Love You?"

Papa God

Limitless life begins the day we let the Limitless One love us. The power of His love is transformative. It is where we find our purpose:

> I ask God from the wealth of his glory to give you power through his Spirit to be strong in your inner selves, and I pray that Christ will make his home in your hearts through faith. I pray that you may have your roots and foundation in love, so that you, together with all God's people, may have the power to understand how broad and long, how high and deep, is Christ's love. Yes, may you come to know his love—although it can never be fully known—and so be completely filled with the very nature of God. To him who by means of his power working in us is able to do so

much more than we can ever ask for, or even think of: to God be the glory in the church and in Christ Jesus for all time, for ever and ever! Amen. (Eph. 3:16–21 GNT)

If there was ever a passage of Scripture that reveals the heartbeat of this book, it's Ephesians 3:16–21. God, in Jesus, wants to reveal and unleash His limitless power in and through you to do more than you ever thought possible, all for His glory, your joy, and to the benefit of this dysfunctional world.

This sounds elementary, yet it is the most difficult thing in the world. How do we know? Just spend five minutes watching the news. Just think about the pain and dysfunction in our lives. Humanity has taken the gifts of God and worshiped them instead of God. This misplaced lust for love and joy outside of God first began in the garden of Eden, and ever since that tragic moment of the great divorce, God has been trying to win our hearts back so we can discover our purpose in being loved by Him. This brokenness results because we try to find love and joy—that is, our purpose—in some*thing* instead of Some*one*: Jesus, the Source of Life. But "In *him* [is] life, and the life [is] the light of men" (John 1:4, emphasis added).

MOVING BEYOND PURPOSELESS: LET GOD REWRITE THE STORY OF YOUR LIFE

I wish I could have been present when Jesus told the story of humanity in the parable of the prodigal son (Luke 15:11–32). It's arguably Jesus' most famous parable. This timeless tale reveals the heart of God and the purpose of humanity. Let's look at that story.

A Father and His Two Sons

Once upon a time there was a loving father who had two sons. The older son was very religious. Externally, he seemed to be a good and devout young man. The younger son was not. Instead of following the rules, he looked for ways to break them. The older son found his purpose in following the rules, not in his father's love. The younger son found his purpose in being rebellious, not in his father's love. Both were in deep need of grace. Each needed to find his true purpose.

The younger, rebellious son, whom I'll call Jacob, disgraced his father one day by saying, "Father, give me the share of the property that will come to me." Under Jewish law, at the death of their father, the elder son, whom I'll call Jude, would get two-thirds of the property, and Jacob would inherit one-third (Deut. 21:17). In this culture a man's standing in the community was based on his land possession. Now, the father, whom we will call John, was not only dishonored by Jacob's request, but he also lost standing in the community because he was losing property.

For Jacob to make this request, he was basically saying, "Hey, old man, I wish you would go ahead and die already." Think of the pain and shame John experienced at the hands of his baby boy. I wonder if he ever thought that one day the baby who had lain on his chest would bring such hurt to his heart.

When you and I take our God-given talents, our intellect, and our circumstances and use them for our own glory, we do exactly the same thing that Jacob, the younger son, did. Basically we are saying, "God, thanks for the gifts, but I will use them for my own purpose, not Yours. Leave me alone. I've got this!"

Surprisingly, the loving father gave his son the property he was to inherit. According to Middle Eastern tradition of that day, John had every right to kick Jacob out of the house without giving him anything! But the father did not throw him out, because love and grace never force relationship; they invite people to find their purpose. God, who is grace and love, pursues and woos us to Himself.

What Happens in Vegas Doesn't Stay in Vegas

John's generosity was sadly lost on Jacob, because he sold the property his father gave him as soon as he could, got a ton of money, and went to the Las Vegas of his day—the far country, where the Gentiles, who did not believe in God, lived. This is symbolic of how you and I attempt to find purpose outside of Jesus.

Jacob deserted his father's provision and protection. He wanted an identity outside of his father's name. However, the Vegas of his day was too fast for him. The women were too wild, and the partying was too much. The boy had gotten in way over his head. His dream life in Vegas turned out to be a nightmare. Instead of joy and fulfillment, Jacob found shame, guilt, and pain.

Years ago, I counseled a young man who grew up in a Christian home, attended a private Christian high school, graduated, and went to a major university. In college, he jumped into a life of premarital sex, partying, drinking, using drugs, and selling drugs. He dropped out of school, and his parents forced him to enter rehab.

A once-bright future was stolen. A mom and dad were heartbroken. A young man was on the verge of death and was now an "atheist." He wanted to find his purpose outside of God the Father's love, and he did. But what he found was a false purpose that gave him a false identity, which literally may have killed him.

But we do this, too, don't we? Moms, do you find your purpose in how your kids turn out? Don't we try to find our purpose in spouses or boyfriends or girlfriends? As the pastor, I, at times, find my purpose in weekly church attendance.

Jacob's true purpose was found at his father's house, in his father's arms, where his father met all his needs. What he didn't realize was that he had all he ever needed at his father's house.

In this nightmare, he found himself working for a Gentile. Jesus' audience would have begun to boo and hiss at this point in the story, because religious Jews considered Gentiles lower than dogs. And as if that were not bad enough, Jacob's job was working with pigs, a ritually unclean animal! A Jew working for a Gentile and feeding pigs was as low as he could get. He not only hit bottom; he smashed through the floor. He was spiritually bankrupt. He was purposeless.

Time to Go Home to Daddy

In the midst of extreme spiritual and physical bankruptcy, with the hurricane of purposelessness tossing him around like a rag doll, "he came to himself" (Luke 15:17). He realized how much his dishonor, pride, and rebellion had cost him, as well as the pain it brought to his daddy's heart. He also recognized that when he'd abandoned his father, he'd abandoned his purpose. He knew he had to go back home and be with his father.

Take note of what the boy did next. He rehearsed a speech that he would give to his father: "Father, I have sinned against heaven and before you. I am no longer worthy to be called your son. Treat me as one of your hired servants" (Luke 15:18–19).

Jacob felt unworthy to be anything but a hired servant!

This is important because an ordinary servant in the first-century Roman world was at least in some sense a member of the family. But the hired servant, like the boy wanted to be, could be fired with a day's notice. When Jacob disassociated himself from his father, he lost his identity and true purpose. As a result, he believed he was worthless. How sad.

A worthless person acts in a worthless way. That's why Jacob was rolling around with pigs. This is what a purposeless life does. It strips us of our God-given dignity.

Ah, don't be too hard on Jacob. This is exactly what you and I do, isn't it? We have all that we need in our Father as well. At our Father's house, in the embrace of His arms, we have every spiritual blessing we will ever need. As Paul told us, "God, the Father of our Lord Jesus Christ, . . . has blessed us with every spiritual blessing in the heavenly realms because we are united with Christ" (Eph. 1:3 NLT).

And yet, we, like the prodigal, seek our purpose in a pigpen!

I remember how empty I was, trying to find my purpose outside of Jesus. So, to try to earn God's love, I became a "hired servant," so to speak, by speaking at high schools to warn students about the dangers of drugs. I started donating money to worthy causes. My wife and I gave more than twenty-five scholarships to at-risk youth so they could go to college. In 1994, while playing for the Indianapolis Colts, I won the RCA Man of the Year Award for community service. Mayor Stephen Goldsmith of Indianapolis even named October 14, 1996, "Derwin Gray Day" for my outstanding community service to the city.

Externally, my religious activities looked good, but on the inside, my soul was constantly asking God, *Is this good enough to make up for my sins? Are You pleased with me now? God, if I do these good things, will I find my purpose?*

Just like Jacob, we want to find a purpose in order to feel good about ourselves, when in reality this deep need is only discovered in God's love. We are called human *be*ings and not human *do*ings for a reason. Beings find purpose from the One who created them. Human *do*ings find their purpose from what they do. And this will never satisfy us. Purpose is not something we earn by being hired servants. Purpose and identity are gifts we receive when we are born from above.

"But to all who believed him and accepted him, he gave the right to become children of God. They are reborn—not with a physical birth resulting from human passion or plan, but a birth that comes from God" (John 1:12–13 NLT).

The Running Father

In the next scene of the prodigal story, we observe John, the father, as he sees Jacob approaching from afar. This means that John had been looking and waiting for his Jacob to return home. The text highlights John's extravagant love when it says, "But while he was still a long way off, his father saw him and felt compassion, and ran and embraced and kissed him" (Luke 15:20).

When I think about my life and all the ways I've ignored God and lusted for a purpose outside of Him, tears well up in my eyes as I picture Him looking over the horizon with compassion in His heart, and watching and waiting for me.

As Jacob got closer and closer, with the instinct of a lovesick daddy, John broke out in a full sprint toward his son. I wonder if Jacob flinched, thinking his father was going to strike him? Instead, his father embraced and kissed him. Instead of blows to the face, he was greeted with kisses. Can you imagine how Jacob felt when he realized that he should be beaten, but instead, he was embraced with grace? Just as

Jacob was meant to be embraced and kissed by His father, our purpose is to be embraced and kissed by our Father.

Let's take a closer look at John, who, by the way, is the star of this story.

Waiting on tiptoe for his younger son, Jacob, to return, first John felt compassion for his son. The word *compassion* means "to suffer with." As Jacob slopped around with pigs, used people, and abused people, his daddy's heart drowned in sorrow over his boy's condition.

On the cross, Jesus carried the weight of all of humanity's condition: our sin, pain, shame, and guilt. Literally, He suffered with every person who has ever existed or will exist. All that heinousness was heaped on Him. He took it all. And was joyful to do so: "Because of the joy awaiting him, he endured the cross, disregarding its shame. Now he is seated in the place of honor beside God's throne" (Heb. 12:2 NLT).

Did you know God looks at you with eyes of compassion and waits for you to return home? What far country are you in right now? Are you seeking your purpose in your job instead of in being loved by God the Papa? Are you basing your identity on your children instead of on your loving Father? Pastor, are your purpose and identity wrapped up in how big or how small your church is instead of in God's love?

Second, John ran to his son. This is very unusual behavior for a distinguished, wealthy Middle Eastern father like John. Men of his stature and in his culture did not run. So why did he? It is quite possible that he ran to protect his son. According to a Jewish custom, when a son disgraced his father and brought shame on him through sinful behavior, the elders of the city would intercept the son before he reached his father. In Jacob's case, they would have taken him to the village center and smashed a pot at his feet, symbolizing his own shame and disgrace. The broken pot was a legal act of banishment. Then the elders would have told him to leave and never return because of his wicked deeds. Or he could have been stoned to death.

How extravagant was John's love for Jacob in preventing this from happening. Can you see John running and reaching his son, embracing and kissing him, while at the same time saying to the elders of the city, "If you stone my son, you must stone me first. This is my son! I love him!" The father would have willingly taken the judgment meant for his son.

When you and I were living misguided, purposeless, selfish lives, Jesus took our judgment on the cross. He experienced the toxic waste of our purposeless lives so we can live in the purpose of His Father's love.

Third, John put a robe on his young son, a ring on his hand, and shoes on his feet. The robe stands for honor. The son had dishonored the father, yet the father honored the son. That's grace.

TIME FOR A NEW LABEL . . . "PURPOSEFUL"

In our American culture, we are pressured into finding purpose in what we do. And based on what we do, we ascend or descend in people's eyes, even our own. But in God's eyes, our place in His heart is forever sealed—we are His children. Everything can be taken from us, but we will always be His. That is our purpose. But if we find our purpose in what we do, who are we when we can't do what we once did? We develop a hired-servant mind-set. We are only useful because of our actions, instead of because of who we are and our purpose of being God's beloved children.

Here are some keys to discovering your life's true purpose:

Key 1: Know That You Wear God's Robe of Honor

You are eternally robed with God's honor.

Do you deserve a robe of honor? Do I? No. You are robed with honor because Jesus gave you His as a gift of grace.

People honor you based on your accomplishments. God the Father honors you—robes you—based on Jesus' accomplishments. Your husband may leave you for a younger woman. Your job may get outsourced to India. But you are forever robed in God's honor.

Key 2: Recognize That You Have God's Authority

The ring in the prodigal story meant that John's authority belonged to Jacob. Jacob had disrespected and lost his father's authority, and yet his father gave it back to him as a gift. That's grace.

Because you are in Christ, God has given you His authority.

We live in a world where people fight and stab one another in the back to gain authority. The perception of power is an intense force that drives us to make decisions that not only aren't healthy for us but also don't bestow any real authority to us. But God's children move to the rhythm of grace; we know that our authority is inherited from our Father, so we can go about life with a humble posture.

Key 3: Understand That You Are God's Child, Not a Hired Servant

The gift of shoes in our story meant that Jacob was John's son, not a hired servant! Jacob wanted to be a hired servant, but John said, "No, you will always be my son." He also honored his son by ordering up a fattened calf, meaning it was time to celebrate! Despite Jacob's betrayal, sin, disrespect, and shame, John threw a huge party and celebrated his son's return. That's grace.

It has always been the kindness of God that brings people to a place of repentance and transformation.

Key 4: Know That God Celebrates You

When you think that what you do through your career, your spouse, or whatever else is the basis for God celebrating you, your real purpose will forever be beyond your grasp. You are God's very own child, and He celebrates you because you are in His beloved Son, Jesus, not because of your accomplishments, your degrees, or anything else. Because you are *in Christ*, God the Father doesn't distinguish you from Jesus. You are united with Jesus. You are His body. Therefore you are forever His beloved.

When my children were babies and could do nothing but pee, poop, eat, and cry, I loved them. Their purpose was to simply let me love them. At night, I would literally sing over them. I drew inspiration from this verse: "The Lord your God is with you; his power gives you victory. The Lord will take delight in you, and in his love he will give you new life. He will sing and be joyful over you, as joyful as people at a festival" (Zeph. 3:17–18 GNT). Right now, the God of the universe, whose sheer presence commands angels to utter in awe, "Holy is the Lord," sings and dances over you like a father who is showing off his babies to friends to admire.

I find it interesting that John totally ignored Jacob's rehearsed speech and his desire to be a hired servant. As Jesus told this story, He was showing us that access to God is not found through religion but through His grace.

Our purpose is to let God the Papa love us, and out of that love He gives us—in Jesus—honor, authority, and adoption. How can we not go into the world and be great at sacred vocations when our hearts are strengthened with these labels?

THE GOD WITHOUT LIMITS

The Greatest Purpose of All: Living as a Child of God

On Easter 2010, Grace and her boyfriend, James, attended one of our services for the first time.

Grace was sexually abused as a teenager, had a horrible relationship with her father, and started experimenting with alcohol and drugs in her teen years. This experimentation turned into a full-blown addiction. Because she broke the law, she got arrested and spent five years in prison.

Grace got married soon after she was released from prison. Then she met James. (James grew up in a middle-class family and was well educated, yet drugs had stolen his life too.) Even though Grace was still married, she moved in with James.

Grace and James had a little girl together.

When James heard Grace say, "Let's go to Transformation Church for Easter," he thought she was crazy. Plus, Transformation Church had a black pastor. James is white and did not like black people.

During our Easter service, Jesus melted Grace's and James's hearts. That day they committed their lives to Jesus. Since that time, Grace has divorced her husband.

One day, after a service, James gave me a huge hug, with tears streaming down his face, and said, "I can't believe I'm in church! I'm so glad someone invited me to Transformation Church! And my pastor is black. I used to be a racist, but Jesus has now transformed my heart."

Grace and James are both now superstar servant leaders at Transformation Church. By serving on various ministry teams, they are giving away the grace that Jesus gave them.

After one service Grace approached me and said, "Pastor Derwin, I'm ready."

"Ready for what?" I asked.

She said, "I'm ready to go back to prison and tell the women that Jesus can transform their lives the way He's transformed mine. Would you help me go back to prison to tell them?"

Needless to say, I said yes.

Grace and James found their purpose: to be loved, embraced, and kissed by God the Papa. After finding their purpose in being loved by Jesus, they have been led by Him to do greater things. Grace began a new career and is getting ready to graduate from a master's program. James is holding a job and providing for his family. Both are drug- and alcohol-free.

And I had the honor of marrying Grace and James in a small, intimate wedding at Transformation Church. Their little girl was the flower girl.

I had something happen to me at the wedding that had never happened before. Grace asked me if I would walk her down the aisle because her father was not involved in her life. I walked Grace down the aisle and gave her away to James, and then I married them.

The Angry Older Brother

What about Jude, the older brother in the prodigal story? Surely Jude would find his purpose because he stayed at his father's house, right? Sadly, Jude was just as far from his father's love as the crazy Jacob.

Jude, the religious brother, was angry that his father would celebrate the return of his brother, Jacob. Jude is the model of a man with a spiritually dead heart but an externally religious life. He had faithfully served his father for years. Listen to his words: "I never disobeyed your command, yet you never gave me a young goat that I might celebrate with my friends. But when this son of yours came, who has devoured your property with prostitutes; you killed the fattened calf for him" (Luke 15:29–30).

Wow. Seriously, dude? Jude, really, you never disobeyed a command?

People who do not understand grace are quick to talk about their "performance" when they feel they've been wronged. "Dad, I always obeyed you," not "Dad, I'm honored to be your son. You have always loved me and given me everything I could ever need." Instead, the older brother showed his true colors by basically telling his dad, "I'm the victim here. You should be celebrating *me*, not your whore-chasing son. I deserve more."

Watch this, now: Jude found his purpose in being good, not in being loved by his daddy. This is what a person who finds their purpose in being good, not in God's goodness, does. Religion says, "I am a good person. Look what I've done." Grace says, "The only goodness in me is Jesus; look at the good thing He's done for me: He loved me."

Even though Jude was religious, he was just as spiritually dead as Jacob. He may have appeared on the outside to be the father's "better" son, but he was just as rotten to the core. Jude was also angry because his brother, Jacob, would now re-inherit his one-third of the property—an additional one-third. This cut into Jude's inheritance, which took away from his identity.

One Found His Purpose; the Other Missed His Purpose

As the story continues, we find Jude standing outside the house during the celebration. Jude had no experience with grace, so he could not give grace to his brother. He only experienced empty religion. Jude's purpose was not found in being loved by his daddy. It was found in what he did for his daddy.

Tragically, many people who follow Jesus live limited lives, like Jude. In a heartbreaking scene, John tells his older son, "All that I have is yours." Because Jude did not serve his father out of love, he couldn't understand why his father was treating his brother with such extravagant love. Both sons were in the "far country"—that is, living purposelessly—and both had abandoned their father's love and purpose for their lives, but in different ways. Jude was a religionist, and Jacob was a wild, hard-partying child. Both were lost. Both tried to save themselves. But only Jacob ultimately let his father save and restore him to his purpose.

Don't you find it ironic that the son who went to Vegas, chased hookers, and partied was the one who experienced grace and was welcomed into the father's house? And that the older, religious brother exiled himself outside the house and missed out on the celebration and his purpose?

TRANSFORMATION MOMENT

Head

Remember this: Your purpose is not found in your career, money, children, spouse, or anything else. Your purpose is to be loved by God.

Heart

Pray:

Papa, there are so many rival gods that are wooing me and warring for my affections. If I give in to them, I will falsely think my purpose is found in these false gods. But Your desire is for me to behold Your beauty and to be transformed by gazing into Your eyes. And my purpose is found in being loved by You. Give me the faith and courage to believe this. In Jesus' name, amen.

Hands

- In the next week, go for a prayer walk and simply ask God to give you the faith and courage to live in your purpose.
- In what things have you sought your purpose? Ask God to help you remember your true purpose.

NINE

FROM WORKER TO WORSHIPER

BY GOD'S DESIGN, WE'RE WORSHIPERS. WORSHIP ISN'T FIRST AN ACTIV-
ity. Worship is first our identity. That means everything we
do and say is the product of worship.

My first job was cutting grass in my neighborhood when
I was fourteen. I love the smell of a freshly mowed lawn. I also
love how a lawn looks when it's manicured to perfection.

If I weren't a pastor, I would seriously consider having a
company called Dewey's Lawn Manicuring Company. Notice
I didn't say lawn mowing, but lawn manicuring. When it
comes to taking care of a lawn, I'm an artist, like Picasso or
Michelangelo.

At nineteen, after my freshman year of college, I got my
next job at the Geneva Steel Mill in Orem, Utah. I worked

with some tough, hard-nosed Utah mountain men. Day in and day out these men showed up to work in difficult conditions to provide for their families. I respected those men.

Working at Geneva Steel made it clear to me that I needed to finish college and that I was not built for working at a steel mill long term.

Eventually, I landed my dream job—the one I'd wanted my entire life—as a professional football player. As you learned earlier in the book, I played for the Indianapolis Colts and the Carolina Panthers. As a pro football player, I learned the power of vision, strategy, preparation, execution, and teamwork.

When I was a little boy, I saw the movie *Trading Places*, in which Eddie Murphy played a character named Billy Ray Valentine. Billy Ray was a street bum. He was taken in by some Chicago investment gurus who were conducting an experiment that involved giving him a new job, a lot of money, and some really, really nice suits.

God used that movie to tattoo my soul. As an adult, I thought, *If Billy Ray, who was poor like me, could get a great job at an investment firm, so can I*. And you may find this surprising, but during my time in the NFL, I took another job, in the off-season. I worked as an intern with an investment firm in Indianapolis, Indiana.

As I learned more about financial planning, I saw that I had a real knack for it. I absorbed everything like a sponge. After reading something once, I got it, and then I could teach it. I ended up helping a lot of my teammates with the Colts get their finances in order.

Following my one season with the Panthers, I worked as an intern with Reebok. The average NFL career lasts only three years, so I wanted to be prepared for the day when I was told by an NFL team, "We no longer need your services."

In 1999, after six years in the NFL, my wife and I started an organization called One Heart at a Time Ministries. My wife ran the day-to-day operations. I traveled the country, speaking at universities, churches, businesses, and just about anywhere else they would let me share the gospel and leadership principles.

I had some amazing adventures throughout the years. I slept on a dorm-room floor at Carson Newman University after preaching at a late-night event. I sang bluegrass praise and worship music at a small church in Kentucky. I preached in stadiums and arenas filled with thousands of people. I preached in a third-world country in a three-hundred-year-old church that was so packed with people that others were crowded outside the church, listening through the windows.

Before planting Transformation Church, I worked for ESPNU and FOX TV in Charlotte as an expert football analyst. And of course now, I'm a pastor.

As I think about the various jobs I've had during my life, my heart is overcome with gratefulness to God for the many ways He has enabled me to provide for my family. But our employment—what we "do"—is not all there is. It's not all we are meant to be.

SCULPTED FOR SOMETHING MORE THAN WORK

Before time began, God placed certain abilities in me and in you, so we could work and "show Him" to our coworkers. While you were in your mother's womb, living and moving and developing, God, like a skilled craftsman, was sculpting you. King David wrote, "Oh yes, you shaped me first inside, then out; you formed me in my mother's womb. I thank you, High God—you're breathtaking! Body and soul, I am marvelously made! I worship in adoration—what a creation! You know me inside and out, you know every bone in my body; you know exactly how I was made, bit by bit, how I was sculpted from nothing into something" (Ps. 139:13–15 MSG).

God gave you a certain personality with certain abilities that would be expressed in a certain way in this world through working a job. And the way you express your personality and abilities through your job should bring you pleasure and Him glory, and it should make a difference in your sphere of influence.

Have you ever built something from scratch? Remember how proud you felt after it was done? All the hard work was worth it. Well, God built you from scratch, so to speak. He took certain aspects of your parents, and your parents' parents, and fashioned you for something in this world, *to worship Him through your work, not to worship your work.*

In our society we regularly define ourselves by our work. When someone asks about who we are, we all too often begin with our job titles. That's the first thing we let people know about us, but it isn't close to being the most important.

To make a point, I'd like you to try an exercise where you look at your life goals. This will help you put into perspective what is really important to you and how you might need to adjust your priorities. As an example, I have inserted my life's vision statement in answer to the questions. Take the time to think about your own answers. As you respond to the questions, also ask yourself, "Is this what God would want for my life? Is this why God made me and put me here?"

CRAFTING A LIFE VISION

Question #1: How do you want to be seen in ten years?

- I want to be seen as a man who loves the Father, Son, and Spirit more than anything else in the universe.
- I want to be seen as a man who fought for the heart of his wife.
- I want to be seen as a papa who fought for Presley's and Jeremiah's hearts as I served and equipped them to glorify God in life.
- I want to be seen as an apostolic pastor-leader who loved, served, and equipped Transformation Church to make God famous in remarkable ways.
- I want to be seen as a man of great faith who embodied the gospel and inspired others to unleash their God-given talents for His glory.

Question #2: What do you want to be known for in ten years?

- I want to be known for launching a multiethnic, multigenerational, mission-shaped church movement through Transformation Church. This will include Transformation Church having multiple campuses with thousands of members and numerous church plants domestically and internationally. It will also include founding and developing a network that trains thousands of pastors in how to execute multiethnic, multigenerational, mission-shaped churches.

Question #3: What do you want your family to be like?

- My wife and I will have a passionate love relationship and partnership in the gospel.

- My children, Presley and Jeremiah, will be close to Jesus, my wife, and me. They will be remarkable, reliable, resilient, and responsible.

Question #4: What makes your heart sing (from a sacred vocation perspective)?

- Leading Transformation Church
- Encouraging pastors
- Helping people realize their potential as Christ-followers for the glory of God (discipleship)
- Helping those who are far from God discover that He is pursuing them to make them His own (evangelism)

Much of this I could do bio-vocationally as a coach, NFL analyst, or financial advisor. At this season of my life, however, leading Transformation Church full-time is the best way to achieve my desired calling.

Question #5: Who in your life will tell you the truth about yourself?

(These people will tell me if my life vision statement matches my gifts.)

- My wife
- The elder-pastors at Transformation Church
- Several pastors to whom I have submitted my life for accountability purposes

As I explained, this is *my* life's vision statement. I keep it close to use as a path to keep me focused on my sacred calling. Making a list like this will do the same for you. Take some time and work through this exercise. Please keep in mind that the younger you are, the more difficult this exercise will be. I'm forty-one at the time of this writing. I've experienced some life.

So what do you do if you are not sure what your sacred calling is?

FINDING THE SACRED IN YOUR WORK

Several years ago, a friend of my mine recommended an amazing young physical therapist to my family and me. After this glowing endorsement, I immediately wanted to go see him. My children are athletes, and I'm an old athlete with a beat-up ex–professional football player body. He was everything our friend said, and more.

He not only has superior knowledge in his area of expertise, but he is a great teacher. As he worked on my children and me, he enthusiastically, patiently, and clearly explained what he was doing in the physical therapy process and why he was doing it. He went about his work as an *artist*. I call him an artist because every detail was significant to him. How he spoke and how he went about physical therapy mattered. And to make the physical rehab experience better, he loved people. He knew the name of each person sitting in the waiting room, and he greeted him or her with a hug or a high five.

Due to my NFL career, I have a bulging disk in my lower back. When you run full speed into another human being over and over again for an extended time, this sort of thing is bound to happen. A few years back, my lower back pain was so bad due to the bulging disk that it took me several minutes to get out of bed each day. This therapist treated me when I was in this condition. I moved at a snail's pace when I slugged my way into his office. I could tell that I mattered to him as a *person*, not simply a profit, as he rehabbed me back to health.

As I was getting better, I asked him, "How often do I need to schedule appointments with you?"

"Derwin, I'm going to give you rehab exercises you can do on your own so you do not have to come back and see me," he said.

"Doc, you do know that the more I come see you, the more money you and your clinic receive."

"Derwin," he said, "I do not do what I do because I make money. I do it because I want to help people and I love what I do."

"Because of that attitude, you will need multiple clinics to keep up with the number of people who will want you to work on them," I told him. "When you love people and add value to their lives, this place will always be overrun with people giving you more business than you can handle."

Since that conversation, my friend has opened up another clinic, and more are on the way.

My friend is a great example of Colossians 3:23: "Whatever you do, work heartily, as for the Lord and not for men." When we work for a paycheck, we limit our lives. When we worship Jesus through our work, God does unlimited things in us and through us that send shock waves throughout eternity.

DON'T JUST WORK—WORK TOWARD YOUR CALLING

Don't find a job so you can simply go to work. That's limiting. Discover your sacred calling. That's limitless.

The ancients used a Latin word to describe what I'm talking about: *vocation*—or a call from God. Our word *vocation* was derived from its root. God doesn't want you to find something to do so you can simply draw a paycheck. He has created and gifted you to express His awesomeness through your calling as a teacher, actor, politician, nurse, or whatever He made you to do.

How many people woke up this morning hating their jobs? How many people only pursue certain jobs because of the money they will make? Life is too short, and you are too important to God and His plans to occupy earth with His kingdom, for you to simply "go to work." He placed a song in your heart that He wants you to dance to. And He wants you to dance in such a way that will cause people to look and say, "Wow! That person loves his job," or "She must be motivated by something more fulfilling than money." God wants you to be motivated by His glory, to worship Him as you work. So how do we discover our calling?

All of Life Is Sacred

All of life is sacred, as we see in this verse: "Whatever you do, do all to the glory of God" (1 Cor. 10:31). For the Christ-follower, there is nothing we do that is "secular." The word *secular* means "without God." Everywhere we go and everything we do is in and with our God. The very God of the universe inhabits us. Therefore, the job you have is your sacred vocation. If you are in school, that is your sacred vocation. One of the ways the enemy of your soul diminishes your imprint on eternity is by getting you to believe the lie that your job is secular and that church stuff is sacred. There is no such thing as the secular/sacred divide.

Whether you are a plumber or a pastor, each of these callings is a sacred vocation. You may be a plumber and pastor simultaneously. Both pastors and plumbers deal with some stinky situations, so that would work well together. (Okay, you know that's funny.)

Life would be so much more eventful, transformative, and purposeful if we saw our jobs as another way to worship our God. Can you imagine waking up in the morning saying, "Wow! Today I get to worship Jesus through my work, display His greatness through my talents, and have the honor of adding value to the lives of the people I interact with"?

Every job is sacred because of our association with Jesus and His mission. Some of the godliest people I know are people in the marketplace. They see themselves as Jesus' ambassadors, representing Him and His kingdom in the workplace, or as I say it, the "worship place." They are not simply a part of the workforce; in Christ they are a part of the "worship force."

God's in the Workforce (Worship Force)

No calling is "holier" than another. Just because someone is called to be a pastor does not necessarily mean he is more spiritually mature than the mechanic, engineer, or investment banker in the congregation. Each person has a role or calling in the Church, which is expressed differently. The key is to understand who we are as God's people. The apostle Peter revealed more life-giving labels: "You are a chosen people. You are royal priests, a holy nation, God's very own possession. As a result, you can show others the goodness of God, for he called you out of the darkness into his wonderful light. 'Once you had no identity as a people; now you are God's people. Once you received no mercy; now you have received God's mercy'" (1 Peter 2:9–10 NLT).

TIME FOR A NEW LABEL . . . "WORSHIPER"

Here are a few keys to worshiping God through your work:

Key 1: Know Your Identity

Come with me as we dive into a great mystery. In this great mystery, we will discover how our identity *in* Christ informs, shapes, and transforms a job into a calling.

You have a new identity—Chosen

The Middle Eastern understanding of the word *chosen* expresses a mission for a community of people to fulfill. Jesus is the Chosen One (Luke 1:35), and He had a mission to establish God's kingdom on earth. Through faith in Jesus, you and I— and every one of His followers all over the world and throughout the ages—now participate in His chosenness and mission.

"God loved us and chose us in Christ" (Eph. 1:4 NLT). His mission now becomes yours and mine. You are chosen in Christ to reflect Him as you worship Him through your work or school.

You have a new identity—Royal Priest

When Jesus wrestled your heart into submission with His grace, and by faith you trusted Him, He gave you another label: "Royal Priest." You are royalty because your Papa is the King. By your new birth, you are born into a royal family. And the King Himself, through His precious Son, Jesus, and by the Spirit's power, has given you His very authority to act on His behalf as you represent Him at your place of work.

You are not working where you are by accident. Your boss did not hire you by chance; the hidden hand of God guided you where you are. In the Old Testament a priest offered sacrifices to God, and those sacrifices were an act of worship. When you and I work with excellence and integrity, our work becomes a sacrificial offering to God, an act of worship. And the fragrance of your worship attracts people to the One you are worshiping.

Here's how you can better worship as you work:

Be prayerful, watchful, and thankful. Wake every morning and pray a simple, yet powerful prayer: "Jesus, today at work [or school] break my heart for people who do not know You. Give me the eyes to see them and the courage and compassion to pursue them with Your love. And Lord, thank You for this job, where I can worship You through my work. Lord, give me the words to share Your gospel of grace clearly."

As I was writing this chapter, I suddenly had to stop typing because a gentleman sat down next to me at my favorite coffee shop. We started talking sports and leadership. He asked me what I do, so I told him that I am now a pastor. As we talked about life, his failed first marriage, and his consulting company, I was able to conversationally share the gospel in the context of everyday life. Then he mentioned that he lives right down the street from Transformation Church. He said he would like to come, so I handed him an "invite card" with the church's information on it.

This scenario happens to me several times a week. Why? I suspect it's because I wake up in the morning and prayerfully ask Jesus to break my heart for people who do not know Him. Then I watch throughout the day for those people. God has strategically positioned you to do this at your job too. We are instructed to "continue steadfastly in prayer, being watchful in it with thanksgiving. At the same time, pray also . . . that God may open . . . a door for the word, to declare the mystery of Christ" (Col. 4:2–4).

Be wise. Have you ever been to a fast-food restaurant where the workers are energetic, excellent, and professional, like the young people at Chick-fil-A? When I see that, especially from teenagers, I tip them and encourage them.

May we work in such a way that we are remarkable,

whether it's flipping burgers, performing surgery, or teaching tenth-grade English! When you worship Jesus through your work, you will be remarkable. You will be excellent. Your coworkers will seek you out as a person of wisdom.

Here's the deal: If we are going to do something, let's do it like no one has ever done it before! Let's do it with passion, intelligence, and integrity because we are worshiping Jesus through our work.

As Christ-followers, may we be the best workers in the organization because we see our work as worship. When you work this way, people who have yet to trust Jesus will seek you out. And this is exactly the reason Jesus placed you where you are. He wants us all to maximize our time at our jobs for His glory and "walk in wisdom toward outsiders, making the best use of the time" (Col. 4:5).

Talk about grace. How does your speech compare to your coworkers'? Does the wisdom of Christ fill their hearts as words flow from your mouth? You can be the one your coworkers go to when they need advice.

One of the reasons I connected with the Naked Preacher is because he spoke in nonreligious terms that I could understand and relate to my everyday life experience. You can do the same for someone. Remember: "Let your speech always be gracious, seasoned with salt, so that you may know how you ought to answer each person" (Col. 4:6).

Remember you are God's possession. Earlier I introduced you to my high school football coach, D. W. Rutledge. What I didn't tell you was that he initially did not want to coach high school football. He wanted to coach college football. As a young coach, his former mentor offered him a job on the coaching staff at a university. This was the opportunity he had been waiting for. One big problem, though: the job did not pay enough for him to support his wife and baby son. He had also been offered a position on the coaching staff for the Converse Judson High School football team, which had a higher salary. So Coach told his mentor that he could not take the job, and that he would be taking the high school position instead. His mentor told him that if he took that job, he would be stuck coaching high school football and most likely would never coach college ball. In that moment, his dreams were shattered.

Coach told me he went home and fell face-first into his bed next to his wife and started sobbing. But after a time of crying, he let the head coach of Converse Judson, Frank Arnold, know that he would take the job at the high school. Coach Rutledge told Coach Arnold, "You will get the best out of me every day for these kids, and I will be the best coach I can possibly be."

Out of his shattered dream, Coach discovered his calling, his sacred vocation. Thousands of players and coaches all over the country have been impacted by Coach Rutledge and his passion to see high school coaches make a difference in the lives of the athletes they coach.

What was Coach's motivation? Why didn't he get mad at God for allowing his dream to be destroyed? Because Coach knew his identity was in Christ. The nanosecond he trusted Jesus as his God, Savior, and King, he renounced any rights to his life as his own. He knew he had been bought with a high price and now belonged to Jesus. "You are not your own," we are reminded, "for you were bought with a price. So glorify God in your body" (1 Cor. 6:19–20).

It's just like Jesus to take Coach's shattered dream and use him as the glue to put my shattered life back together. And not just my life but the lives of many young men like me. Coach Rutledge was an artist at coaching. He worked with a passion and with excellence, and his motivation was about something greater than winning football games. He wanted young men to win the game of life. He worshiped Jesus through his work. He believed his job mattered to Jesus and His kingdom. And so does your job. No matter how small and insignificant you think your job is, it isn't to Jesus. What you see as inconsequential, God sees as strategic to His kingdom advancing.

THE GOD WITHOUT LIMITS

Just a Woman at Work

While I played for the Indianapolis Colts, my wife worked at a health clinic in downtown Indianapolis. A coworker befriended my wife, and they really connected. Vicki saw something in her that was "different." Whatever this difference was, it attracted my wife to her.

One day while working together, this woman asked my wife a simple question that forever changed the course of our lives. She and my wife were sitting in their offices and she asked, "Are you a Christian?"

"Yes, I believe in God," answered Vicki.

With a heart full of love, her friend said, "Well, being a Christian is more than just believing in God. It means that you trust Jesus as your Lord and Savior. It means you believe that Jesus died for your sins and rose from the dead three days later to give you eternal life as a gift and make you a part of His family called the Church."

My wife listened to her coworker because her friend had earned the right to be heard by the way she lived her life. This woman was very influential in my wife coming to faith. As Jesus was transforming Vicki through this woman's influence, I saw my wife become a different person right before my eyes. I wanted what my wife had, and eventually, I came to faith too.

I'm so thankful a woman worshiped Jesus through her work and that the fragrance of that worship attracted my wife. God has used Vicki and me to touch millions of lives over the years through our roles speaking and writing. And God used a person who took her identity as a royal priest seriously.

The greatest missionary force in America is the Christ-follower in the workforce, or "worship force." Just imagine: right now, at your job or school, there is a person who will be attracted to Jesus as you worship Him through your work. Are you kidding me? How glorious is that! You can impact your coworkers the way the woman at my wife's job influenced her.

Key 2: Know Your Calling

Perhaps you are thinking, *Pastor Derwin, I get what you are saying. But how do I find my calling?*

When I disciple people and walk them through discovering their sacred vocations, I take them through the "Crafting a Life's Vision" exercise we covered earlier. Crafting a life's vision is the first and most important step in discovering your calling because it forces you to sit down with God and look at what you want from life and how that lines up with what we know from His Word that He wants for us.

But putting that into practice takes time. You can start incrementally as you go through each day, in each encounter, finding a way to make a difference and changing the way you handle yourself in business and in life.

The Airport

I've logged quite a few miles flying over the years, traveling the country and preaching at various conferences, churches, and business gatherings. As I travel from one city to the next, I often fly into an airport and have a layover before I board another plane to reach my final destination.

Discovering your sacred vocation is like flying from one city to the next, with a layover in between. You may start in one career, spend some time there, learn some things, and then move on, just as I spent a summer working at Geneva Steel in Orem, Utah. I learned some things there that have helped me in life, but Geneva Steel was not my final destination. It was just a layover where I learned and grew as a man.

Just because your current job may be a layover, however, doesn't mean that you do not give your all for the glory of God. Often people were created for something else, but because they were not faithful in their "layover season," the layover became their final destination. Be faithful with the job you have now because you are worshiping Jesus through your work.

But what if you are at a job that you do not like, and you just can't understand why God would place you there? What then? I want to share a story with you that will help you walk through this difficult season.

Max and Me

Several years ago, when my son, Jeremiah, was seven, I coached his flag football team. One of his teammates was an adorable little guy named Max. Max is never going to be mistaken for the next biggest, meanest football player! He is the kind of young man who, if an ambulance went screaming by the field, would stop practice and say, "Let's pray." I love me some Max.

During one of our games, Max wanted to play another position instead of the position I had assigned to him. He saw that his teammates were scoring touchdowns, and he wanted to do what they were doing. So he persistently let me know that he was not satisfied with the position I had him playing.

Max stopped trusting that I knew what was best for him. But as his coach, with NFL experience, I knew the position where Max would have the most success, given the ability he had. More important, I loved Max and wanted him to succeed. So at halftime, he shed some tears. He was mad at me. Through his tears, I told Max, "Trust me! I have you in the perfect position to make an interception. Trust me! If you do your assignment with maximum effort, like you've been coached, you will get an interception in this game to help us win. Trust me, Max. I love you!"

Later in the game, Max got an interception and returned it for a touchdown. His teammates lifted him up and celebrated his success. I ran from the other end of the field and lifted him up too. Now I was crying.

MARINATE ON THAT!

The next time you look around and find yourself doubting if God loves you because you feel that you are not in the job for which you were created, just remember that your past, present, and future are held in the nail-pierced hands of Jesus; He knows the best position for you to be in. You can trust Him, even when you don't understand.

Even if you are not in your ideal job, be faithful and trust God. Do your best for His glory. Before time began, God sculpted you with His very own hands of grace and glory to do something special. Worship Him through your work. You are not just a worker. That's limiting. You are a worshiper. That's limitless.

TRANSFORMATION MOMENT

Head

Remember: Your job is not just a means to make money. Your job is an opportunity to make Jesus famous as you worship Him through your work.

Heart

Pray:

Father, open my eyes to the joy of seeing my work as a means of worship! May the joy that comes from making You famous in and through my work overflow from my heart so much that my coworkers notice You in me. Empower me to be remarkable at what I do in Your name. And Father, may many of my coworkers come to faith as a result of my influence at work. In Jesus' name, amen.

Hands

- Craft a life vision statement answering the five questions in this chapter.
- Share it with someone you trust who will tell you the truth. Does your life vision statement match your abilities?

TEN

FROM FAILURE TO FAITHFUL

Failure is the key to success; each mistake teaches us something.[1]

—**Morihei Ueshiba**

EVER HAVE A REALLY BIG DREAM? HAVE YOU EVER ACCOMPLISHED THAT big dream and then blew it?

In 1994, I was the starting strong safety for the Indianapolis Colts. For my entire life, I had wanted to be a starter in the NFL, and now I was, in just my second year as a professional. I was living the dream . . . for a while.

During a particular game against Tampa Bay, I observed that the Buccaneers were running a certain play that I thought I could defend. Actually, I thought I could defend the play so well that I would be on ESPN later that night and everyone would see me as the hero of the game. After all, in the previous game, which was my first NFL start, I had played great and had led my team in tackles.

During one of the breaks in the game, I said to my defensive back coach, "I know what play they are running. I can defend it."

What happened next is forever painted into my mind as a mural of failure. Coach said, "Derwin, take care of your responsibility, and let your teammates do their jobs. They can make the play."

With a nod of my head, I let my coach know that I understood. But in my heart, I said, *Screw that. I'm going to make a play on the ball.* Because I was young, inexperienced, and bursting with pride, little did I know that Tampa Bay was setting me up. They kept running the same play over and over to bait me so I would get out of position.

The next time we took the field, I quickly saw what play they were going to execute, or so I thought. When I reacted to the play I thought they were going to execute, they instead ran another play. I was badly out of position. I remember chasing a Tampa Bay football player named Jackie Harris as he ran for a touchdown. I let my team down. I failed. And I was definitely on ESPN later that night, but not for the reason I wanted to be.

In one week, I went from leading the team in tackles to being one of the main causes we lost the game. Personally, I lost more than just the game. I lost the trust of my teammates and the trust of the coaches.

For the remainder of my career with the Colts, the coaches never trusted me with that level of responsibility again. Every year after that 1994 season, the coaches drafted college players to take my job. And every year I fought them off like a male lion fighting to keep his pride.

I lost millions of dollars too. Had I played up to my potential the remainder of the season, it would have placed me in a good position to sign a new, much bigger contract.

Worst of all, I lost my confidence. In one week, I went from "Dang, this NFL stuff is easy! I'm the leading tackler on the team!" to "I'm not sure I can do this. Am I good enough to play at this level?" The rest of the 1994 season was a disaster for me. And there was no one to blame but me. Pride blinded me so badly that I tried to blame others for my lack of discipline.

I failed. But I wasn't a failure. What I didn't know in my early twenties was that *the road to success goes through a dark valley called failure.* God placed the seeds of success in my failure that day to make me the man and leader I am today. And that failure would prepare me to live a life of faithfulness.

Right now, my friend, in your greatest failure, God is preparing you for your future success.

FAILURE DOESN'T HAVE TO DEFINE YOU

Do any of these scenarios sound familiar?

Has unforgiveness toward your spouse grown into a toxin-laden weed called resentment and planted deep roots in your heart? Maybe now you are flirting with the young, attractive fitness instructor at the YMCA. It may seem harmless. But what starts out as harmless will grow and grow into something more, and you will become someone you never thought you would be. Eventually you come home and tell your wife, "I no longer love you. I'm moving out at the end of the week." You have failed.

You thought the grass was greener in another lawn, but once you got there, you realized it was on top of a stinky, filthy septic tank. You have crushed your wife and children. And now you see the error of your ways, and guilt is gnawing at your heart like a dog chewing on a bone.

Or maybe you had your dream job, but lost it because of insecurity. Instead of getting help when you were in over your head, you unsuccessfully tried to cover up your mistakes by lying. By the time your mistakes were found out, too many people were hurt and the company was damaged. You were fired from your dream job.

Maybe you were a pastor of a thriving, dynamic church, but you have a secret. You are addicted to pornography or another sinful behavior, and you've lost it all because of your lack of self-control.

Whatever your circumstances, I'm sure you have experienced a failure. But one of the most limiting things you can do is see yourself *as* a failure. Failure doesn't have to define you.

I wonder how many people live tortured lives because of past failures. The failure in their past steals their today. What if I told you that your greatest failure may be the turning point in your life?

FAILURE ISN'T THE END OF THE ROAD

Go to a concert or a big sports event, and you will be able to feel it—the atmosphere bursts with anticipation.

Around the time of Jesus, the atmosphere was bursting with anticipation as well. Instead of waiting for a concert, Jews were waiting for the Messiah to come and rescue them from the pagan Roman occupiers.

At the same time, a man by the name of John, who ate locusts and dressed in a suit made from camel hair, was baptizing people at the Jordan River. John the Baptist, as he was known, was a rock star. Crowds followed him wherever he went. He was a one-man show.

The common people loved John because he ticked off the upper-class religious establishment. John would cuss them out in religious language by calling them a "brood of vipers" (Matt. 3:7).

One day while John was baptizing people at the Jordan River, he uttered the words that he had waited his whole life to say, "Behold, the Lamb of God, who takes away the sins of the world!" (John 1:29). And when he said those words, his disciples left him and followed the Lamb of God, Jesus.

John always knew he was not the main attraction but just the warm-up act. *He knew who he was and what his mission was.* John knew his role was to prepare the way of the Lord, so he did not take it personally when the masses turned and followed Jesus. He did not see himself as a failure of a prophet or leader. If we take a lesson from John, then when we know who we are and what our mission is, we will not be insecure when the crowd stops following us to follow someone else.

WHO WAS ANDREW?

One of John's disciples who later followed Jesus was a fisherman named Andrew. As Andrew and another disciple of John the Baptist began to follow Jesus, Jesus looked back at them and said, "What do you want?" (John 1:38 NLT). On the surface that sounds cold, but that was typical first-century rabbi language. Jesus was asking Andrew and the other disciple, "What do you want out of life?"

The disciples said, "Rabbi (which means 'Teacher'), where are you staying?" but they were really asking, "Where can I sit at your feet and learn from you?"

Jesus said, "Come and see" (v. 39 NLT).

When Jesus said, "Come and see," it meant serious business. To follow a rabbi meant a total life commitment. In essence, Jesus was saying, "Do you know what you are asking? You are signing up to have My thoughts become yours. You are signing up to have My mission become your mission. You are signing up for My life to become your life." Jesus was inviting Andrew into a life of transformation.

And He is inviting you and me into a life of transformation. He wants us to follow Him so closely that His greatness rubs off on us. "Students are not greater than their teacher," He said. "But the student who is fully trained will become like the teacher" (Luke 6:40 NLT). As Andrew decided to follow Jesus, he was taking an intentional step toward being transformed by immersing himself in the life of the rabbi Jesus.

"I'VE FOUND THE MESSIAH!"

Andrew trusted John the Baptist. So when John said, "Behold the Lamb of God, who takes away the sins of the world!" Andrew knew he was saying, "The King of the kingdom has arrived in human form. Israel's Messiah has come to make all the sad things untrue. The King of the kingdom of God has come to rule and reign among His people."

Once Andrew believed Jesus was Israel's long-awaited Messiah, he went and got his brother, Simon, to meet Jesus. (Perhaps you know Simon better as Peter.) Simon went on to become one of the great heroes of the Bible. But what about Andrew? Basically, the only thing we know about him is that he was one of John the Baptist's disciples who first followed Jesus. The most famous thing Andrew ever did was introduce Simon to Jesus.

Here is something to marinate in: What if the greatest thing you ever did was make someone else great? No newspaper articles or TV show appearances. No thousands of followers on Twitter or scores of friends on Facebook. As a matter of fact, what if you aren't remembered at all, but the people you introduce to the Messiah go on to do epic things in Jesus' name? Are you okay with being unrecognized and unacknowledged?

Let me encourage you. No one may see the behind-the-scenes work Jesus is doing through you, but God the Father sees. And He's cheering you on. He may even at times call an angel to His side and say, "Look at My child serving humbly, effectively, and beautifully. Well done, good and faithful servant."

TO WHOSE NAME DO YOU ANSWER?

The name you embrace is the name you will live by.

In high school, I chose not to pursue challenging classes. Why should I? When I was a little boy, one of my mom's boyfriends called me dumb. And to compound matters, no one at home could help me with my homework, since no one in my immediate family had made it through high school. Plus, I couldn't ask questions in class because I stuttered. Who wants to be laughed at in class?

Because of these experiences, deep in my heart the name "Dumb" echoed loudly. I answered to the name Dumb. That *was* a label I wore. When I think about how limiting this was, I find it hard to even imagine that I once believed that nonsense. But sometimes labels are stitched so deeply in our hearts that we don't even know the lies we believe.

What name do you answer to? Divorced? Molested? Abandoned? Fatherless? Ugly? Fatty? Fearful?

THE GOD WITHOUT LIMITS

"Failures" Become Faithful Followers

When I was in sixth grade, the school gave students a test to see who would be given an opportunity to join the school's band. I remember taking that test and thinking, *Man, this music stuff just doesn't make sense.* A few weeks went by, and some of my classmates were invited to join the band. I remember feeling like a loser because I didn't get picked. I didn't measure up.

Do you ever feel like a loser who doesn't measure up?

Did you know that Jesus only asks losers to be His disciples? All Jesus' disciples would have been considered losers by their culture. No rabbi in the first-century Jewish world would have chosen Peter or any of the other guys to be his followers.

Let me give you some historical context to grasp the significance of Jesus choosing His "loser" disciples. For Jewish people of the first century, the education of their children was not just important; it was the key means of survival as the people of God.[2] The child's education was shaped by God's story; it centered on the first five books of the Bible, called the Torah. The Jewish historian Josephus said, "Above all else, we pride ourselves on the education of our children."[3]

Beginning at age six in *Bet Sefer*, which means "House of the Book,"[4] Jewish children would attend studies in a local synagogue and be taught by the local rabbi. They would also begin memorizing the Torah (Genesis, Exodus, Leviticus, Numbers, and Deuteronomy).

By age ten, the students would move to the next level of their education, called *Bet Talmud*, which means "House of Learning"[5] and continue until age fourteen. By this time the student would have memorized all thirty-nine books of the Old Testament. The best and brightest students would have separated themselves from the not-so-smart kids and continued their education. The not-so-bright would be encouraged to learn the family trade. If your family made shoes, you would begin to apprentice with your father to carry on the shoe-making trade.[6]

At the end of *Bet Talmud*, only the top students were still continuing their education. The "losers" were now immersed in the family trade and starting families of their own. The students who showed an aptitude for the Scriptures would find a well-known rabbi and apply to be his *talmidim* (disciple).[7] The goal of discipleship was to become like the rabbi they chose to follow. A student would present himself to a well-known rabbi and say, "I want to become a disciple of yours." The rabbi would then interview the applicant to see if he was good enough, if the kid had what it took to become like him. If the rabbi approved his application, the disciple would abandon everything and follow the rabbi wherever he went.

Jesus took the very opposite approach. Instead of waiting for the best of the best to apply to be His students, He went after the losers and asked them to become His followers. Jesus was a rabbi who chose the "failures" and "losers" to be His disciples.

Jesus dumbfounded the world and transformed the course of history through twelve "failures."

If you are reading this book and feel like a loser, you're in luck! Jesus is looking for you. He still transforms failures into faithful disciples who change the course of history.

TIME FOR A NEW LABEL . . . "FAITHFUL"

God likes to give people new names. Think of Jacob-turned Israel. And think of Simon: "Then Andrew brought Simon to meet Jesus. Looking intently at Simon, Jesus said, 'Your name is Simon, son of John—but you will be called Cephas' (which means 'Peter')" (John 1:42 NLT).

God wants to give you a new name too: Faithful. Here are some keys to moving from Failure to Faithful:

Key 1: Realize That the Name You Answer to Is the Name You Will Live By

Andrew brought his brother, Simon, to Jesus. And Jesus looked intently into the eyes of Simon and said, "You will be called Peter, the Rock." As I picture this scene, I see Jesus looking at Simon and Andrew walking toward Him from a distance. I see Jesus smiling at first. Then Jesus' smile dissipates and His eyes began to tear up because He sees the day when Peter (Simon), in fear, will deny that he ever knew Jesus. He knew how that denial would break Peter's heart. But as Simon gets closer, the tears of sorrow are transformed into tears of joy because now He sees the day when Peter will be one of the primary leaders of the greatest movement the world has ever seen, Christianity.

Jesus says to Simon, "I will call you Peter, the Rock."

It takes time to learn how to live by the new name Jesus gives you. Be patient with yourself. Spiritual maturity cannot be microwaved; it's more like a slow-marinating process. Train your ears to hear Jesus call you by your new name in the midst of a loud and noisy world that calls you by your old one.

Over the next three years, Jesus would teach Peter how to answer to his new name, which would eventually lead Peter to a new life—a limitless life. Who would have ever known that a simple fisherman would preach the sermon that birthed the Church? Who knew? Jesus. Jesus takes limited people and accomplishes the unlimited.

Drop Your Nets

When Jesus called Peter to be one of His disciples, Peter was shocked. A rabbi did not call a disciple, much less someone like him. We get this story in Matthew:

> While walking by the Sea of Galilee, he saw two brothers, Simon (who is called Peter) and Andrew his brother, casting a net into the sea, for they were fishermen. And he said to them, "Follow me, and I will make you fishers of men." Immediately they left their nets and followed him. And going on from there he saw two other brothers, James the son of Zebedee and John his brother, in the boat with Zebedee their father, mending their nets, and he called them. Immediately they left the boat and their father and followed him. (4:18–22)

When Jesus called Andrew and Peter, they immediately dropped their nets and followed Him. Perhaps for the first time, Peter didn't see himself as a loser. Thoughts that someone believed in him may have run through his mind. Maybe he remembered the painful days when he'd realized through his educational development that he wasn't as smart as the kids who were disciple potential. Perhaps he looked into the eyes of his father, who had taught him to fish, and no word was spoken, but Peter's father looked at him in such a way as to say, *Son, it's okay. Go with the rabbi. I'm so proud of you. Go.*

Can you imagine Peter and Andrew's daddy going home to their mother and saying, "Sweetheart, you will never believe this! A rabbi called our sons to follow Him. Can you believe it? This rabbi believes in our sons. He believes they can be like Him."

Andrew and Peter dropped their nets. They left their

daddy and followed Jesus. And as they did, they also left their former identity to find a new one, forged by Jesus.

This story resonates deeply with me because it's my life. I come from a family brutalized by drugs, a lack of education, and criminal activity. My childhood friends laughed at my house because it was a disaster. And as you learned earlier in the book, I did not go to church growing up. I was spiritually lost!

I didn't even own a Bible my first years in the NFL. But when the team would travel and stay in hotels, I did notice that there were Gideon Bibles in the rooms. One day I decided to steal one. It wasn't until I became a Christ-follower that I realized the Gideons intentionally placed the Bibles in hotel rooms so people could take them for free!

As I look at my life and all the things God has done, I cry. How could I not drop my nets and follow Jesus too? Have you dropped your nets to follow Him? Or do you think you are unqualified? You're *not* qualified to follow Him. And neither am I. But the true rabbi, Jesus, is calling losers and failures—like us.

Key 2: Be Humble—Humility Lets Jesus Transform You into a Winner

Jesus can do anything, but we often make it really hard for Him to work in our lives when we refuse to let go of the reins, thinking we can handle life on our own. But Jesus said, "Blessed are those who recognize they are spiritually helpless. The kingdom of heaven belongs to them" (Matt. 5:3 GW).

Bold . . . but Not Necessarily Humble

Peter was bold. He was a take-action kind of guy. You never had to guess what was on his mind. Peter is known for saying some profound things to Jesus:

"Lord, to whom shall we go? You have the words of eternal life, and we have believed, and have come to know, that you are the Holy One of God." (John 6:68–69)

"You are the Christ, the Son of the living God." (Matt. 16:16)

When other disciples were deserting Jesus, Peter knew that only Jesus had the words of eternal life. When people were asking the identity of Jesus, it was Peter who said, "You are the Christ [Messiah], the Son of the living God."

As the reality of the reason why Jesus came to earth was bearing down on Him, He told His disciples during a Passover meal, "One of you will betray me." The disciples were sorrowful.

They later walked to the Mount of Olives, where Jesus next told them they would all abandon Him that night.

Then Peter boldly and fearlessly told Jesus, "Though they all fall away because of you, I will never fall away" (Matt. 26:33).

Let's just pause for a moment. I applaud Peter's boldness, but the reality is this: the very One whom Peter had affirmed as the Son of God, the Messiah, with the same mouth Peter, in so many words, was now calling a liar! Peter had seen Jesus walk on water, heal demon-possessed people, and tell a storm to stop, and it obeyed. But Peter was now telling Him, "What You're saying is *not* going to happen!" This is called pride. And pride is what ultimately led to Peter's greatest failure. It will lead to our greatest failures too.

Key 3: Remember That Your Weaknesses Attract Jesus' Strength

Peter was incredibly prideful. He wanted to believe he was in control. Even in the midst of Peter's pride, Jesus, who knows and sees all things, knew and saw the day Peter would be so broken, so devastated, that his illusions of strength would be gone. And his heart would be open to let Jesus' strength be his own. Let's look at their exchange.

Jesus looked Peter in the eyes and told him, "Simon, Simon, behold, Satan demanded to have you, that he might sift you like wheat, but I have prayed for you that your faith may not fail. And when you have turned again, strengthen your brothers" (Luke 22:31–32).

And Peter responded to Jesus with more pride. Instead of saying something like, "Lord, please help me remain faithful during this time of sifting," he said, "Lord, I am ready to go with you both to prison and to death" (Luke 22:33).

But Jesus told him, "Truly, I tell you, this very night, before the rooster crows twice, you will deny me three times" (Mark 14:30).

Then Peter came back with, "Even if I must die with you, I will not deny you!" (Matt. 26:35).

I went through something similar until I came to a brutal realization. One day I understood that, on my own, I could not be the husband my wife needed, could not be the father my kids needed, and could not lead Transformation Church as they needed. Only then was I humble enough to let Jesus be my strength. Weakness is our strength.

Key 4: Know That Jesus Doesn't Give Up on You, Even When You Fail Him

Peter and the other disciples failed to stand watch with Him in the Garden of Gethsemane. He was soon betrayed by a kiss from Judas and taken into custody by His enemies.

As Jesus was led to a mock trial in the middle of the night, Peter followed close behind.

But not so close as to actually be identified with Jesus.

Crucified at a Campfire

Peter was outside the courtyard where Jesus was being held. He was warming himself by a campfire. And as the heat warmed him, a slave girl said to Peter, "Hey, you were with Jesus the Galilean."

Peter replied, "I don't know this man." That was the first denial.

Then Peter decided to move to the entrance of the courtyard of the high priest. There, another slave girl said, "Hey, you were with this Jesus from Nazareth." Again Peter denied that He knew Jesus. But this time he added an oath to his denial, to show how ridiculous her conclusion was. That was the second denial.

Soon more bystanders said to Peter, "There is no doubt you were with Jesus. Your accent gives you away." This time Peter invoked a curse upon himself and swore that he did not know Jesus! That was the third denial. And at that moment, Peter remembered what Jesus had said: "Before the rooster crows, you will deny me three times" (Matt. 26:75).

Peter left and cried his broken heart out.

Have you been where Peter was—brokenhearted and feeling like a failure? I have. Maybe it was an affair you said you would never have. Maybe you told Jesus you would remain a virgin until you were married. Or maybe you finally reached the corner office with your name on the door, but you backstabbed and deceived your way to the top. Failure hurts, doesn't it?

But, in God's way of doing things, He redeems our failures and out of the burning ashes can arise a man or woman of God who is ready to transform the world. Remember what Jesus said to Peter: "Simon, Simon, behold, Satan demanded to have you, that he might sift you like wheat, but I have prayed for you that your faith may not fail. And when you have turned again, strengthen your brothers" (Luke 22:31–32).

In the midst of Peter's soon-coming failure, Jesus saw when Peter would return. In the midst of failures, Jesus provides hope for our return too.

Key 5: Remember That Your Failures Can Be Transformed into Triumphs

Jesus prayed for Peter when Satan sifted him like wheat.

Sifting is a brutal process. But just as wheat must be sifted to get to the good stuff, you and I must be sifted to bring out the best in us. Jesus saw what would happen at the end of the failures as Peter was sifted. Only after the sifting would Simon be ready to live up to his new name, Peter. Only then would he be humble enough to be one of the leaders in the greatest force the world would ever see—the Church of Jesus Christ!

Maybe you are being sifted right now. If so, read on.

MARINATE ON THAT!

God is using Satan as a sifting tool to bring out the good stuff in you! Whatever God allows Satan to do to you is happening to bring Jesus out of you, so He can be displayed through you. You will win. Always.

Resurrection at a Campfire

At the campfire in the courtyard, Simon was being burned away and crucified so the "Peter," or rock, that Jesus had birthed in him could be resurrected. Jesus was publicly humiliated. He was savagely flogged naked before jeering crowds. His beard was pulled out. His head was crowned with thorns. His face was covered with soldiers' spit, which mingled with the blood that flooded down Jesus' face. He was paraded through the streets of Jerusalem with a beam that dug into the ripped flesh on His mutilated back. He was crucified between two thieves. He died a long, humiliating death at the hands of the very people He came to rescue. And His last words were, "It is finished."

For three days, Jesus' disciples went back to what they did best. Simon went back to fishing. I'm sure he thought he would live the rest of his life as a failure.

Ever thought your greatest failure would be the last chapter penned in your book of life?

All hell celebrated Jesus' death, until early Sunday morning, when the stone was rolled away from Jesus' tomb. By the way, the stone was not rolled away so Jesus could get out; it was rolled away so the disciples could look in to see that Jesus had risen from the dead, as He said He would.

The women, who visited the tomb first, came back and told Peter what had happened. And Peter took off running to the tomb. But John, a younger disciple, beat Peter to the empty tomb. I wonder what went through Peter's mind when he stooped down and peered in, only to find nothing but Jesus' linen clothes. One day I'll ask him.

Soon Peter was fishing, with no luck at all, and a voice that sounded somewhat familiar said, "Cast your nets to the other side." The nets became so full that the disciples couldn't get them in the boat!

John, one of the disciples, screamed, "It is the Lord!"

Peter's heart leapt! Could it be Jesus? Could it really be Him? And when he realized it was Jesus, Peter threw himself into the water and swam to shore. On the shore, Jesus, with nail-pierced hands, was grilling some fish.

Let's eavesdrop on Jesus' conversation with Peter:

When they had finished breakfast, Jesus said to Simon Peter, "Simon, son of John, do you love me more than these?" He said to him, "Yes, Lord; You know that I love you." He said to him, "Feed my lambs." He said to him a second time, "Simon, son of John, do you love me?" He said to him, "Yes, Lord; you know that I love you." He said to him, "Tend my sheep." He said to him the third time, "Simon, son of John, do you love me?" Peter was grieved because he said to him the third time, "Do you love me?" and he said to him, "Lord, you know everything; you know that I love you." Jesus said to him, "Feed my sheep. Truly, truly, I say to you, when you were young, you used to dress yourself and walk wherever you wanted, but when you are old, you will stretch out your hands, and another will dress you and carry you where you do not want to go." (This he said to show by what kind of death he was to glorify God.) And after saying this he said to him, "Follow me." (John 21:15–19)

At a campfire just three days earlier, Simon had denied that he ever knew Jesus—three times. With those denials, Simon Peter was symbolically crucified and killed as he experienced failure. Now, at another camp, Simon Peter was resurrected as Jesus asked him three times, "Do you love me?" And Peter said, "Lord, you know everything; you know that I love you." Did you catch that?

Finally, after he'd been sifted and humbled by his epic failure, Peter was ready to follow Jesus and experience limitless life. How do we know? Because he said, "Lord, *you* know everything." Simon the failure was ready to be Peter the faithful.

Peter is now a hero of the faith. He went on to advance the kingdom of God in profound ways.

His failure could have defined and limited his life. But when you follow Jesus, the God of the resurrection, failure becomes a platform that catapults you into limitless life. Your best days are ahead.

In Christ, you are limitless.

TRANSFORMATION MOMENT

Head

Your failure is not the end of you. In God's way of doing things, your failure becomes the foundation for future success and future faithfulness for His glory, your joy, and the benefit of our broken world.

Heart

Pray:

Papa God, I'm so thankful that my failures are not the end of me. Today I want to thank You for redeeming every one of my failures and using them to bring the best of Your Son, Jesus, out of me. By the Spirit's power, I will be faithful. I look forward to the great and glorious ways You will make Yourself famous in me and through me. In Jesus' name, amen.

Hands

- Go make *His-story*! You are without limits!

CONCLUSION

CAN YOU HEAR IT? SLOW DOWN; QUIET YOUR SOUL . . . NOW CAN YOU hear it?

The sound you hear is Jesus ripping the labels off your soul. When Jesus removes deep, ingrained labels from our hearts, it hurts. But it's a good hurt, a hurt that heals us. Like recovery from a major surgery, there is a season of soreness in our souls. But with each passing day of spiritual rehab, not only do we regain strength, we regain it from a source beyond us, from Jesus Himself.

Jesus is our new label. His life becomes ours. God the Father, through the Spirit's power, has sewn our lives into His, and His life into ours. "For you died to this life, and your real life is hidden with Christ in God. And when Christ, who is your life, is revealed to the whole world, you will share in all his glory" (Col. 3:3–4 NLT).

You are ready to be and do everything that God has created you to be and do. Because of the unlimited One, you, too, are *without limits.*

ACKNOWLEDGMENTS

I'M OFTEN ASKED, "HOW LONG DOES IT TAKE TO WRITE A BOOK?" I respond by saying, "It takes a lifetime." I may have put pen to paper to write *Limitless Life*, but Jesus used a lot of people to write His story of grace in my life. Here are a few I'd like to thank:

My wife, my best friend, and the love of my life, Vicki, who believes in me more than anyone else on the planet. She is simply remarkable in every way.

My daughter, Presley, my beautiful "brown-eyed princess"; and my son, Jeremiah, the "Big Bull." Presley and Jeremiah, I have no doubt that the world will be better because of you. You are loved by Jesus, called by Jesus, and empowered by Jesus. You are limitless.

The elder-pastors of Transformation Church, the incredible leaders of Transformation Church, and the Transformation Church congregation, whom I affectionately call "Transformers." Transformers, you bring out the best in me. I pray I bless you as much as you bless me.

My friends Chris McGinn, Janene MacIvor, Cara Highsmith, and the Thomas Nelson editorial team, for your superb editorial skills. You guys are editorial ninjas!

Joel Miller of Thomas Nelson, for believing in the *Limitless Life* message.

My super-agent, Esther Fedorkevich, who told me, "Derwin, you are a great writer! I'm getting you a book deal! Keep writing."

And finally, and most important, I want to thank my God and King, Jesus. I could write for all eternity and still not have enough words to describe how beautiful He is and how much He means to me. So the best I can do is quote the apostle Paul,

> But whatever gain I had, I counted as loss for the sake of Christ. Indeed, I count everything as loss because of the surpassing worth of knowing Christ Jesus my Lord. For his sake I have suffered the loss of all things and count them as rubbish, in order that I may gain Christ and be found in him, not having a righteousness of my own that comes from the law, but that which comes through faith in Christ, the righteousness from God that depends on faith. (Phil. 3:7–9).

NOTES

Chapter 1: From Afraid to Courageous

1. "Mandela at 90: Mandela in His Own Words," CNN.com, June 26, 2008, http://edition.cnn.com/2008/WORLD /africa/06/24/mandela.quotes/index.html.
2. Muhammad Ali, http://www.chiff.com/recreation/sports /sports-stars/muhammad-ali.htm.
3. Martin Luther King Jr., "Antidotes for Fear" (sermon) in *Strength to Love*, Fortress Press Gift ed. (Cleveland: Collins + World, 1977; Minneapolis: Fortress, 2010), 124. Citation is from the Fortress edition.
4. Christian Newswire, "Outreach Magazine Special Report: 100 Largest and Fastest-Growing U.S. Churches," September 13, 2011, http://www.christiannewswire.com /news/5135517754.html.

Chapter 3: From Mess to Masterpiece

1. Steve Jobs, commencement address at Stanford University
   (Stanford, CA), June 12, 2005. The text of this address can
   be viewed in the *Stanford Report* website dated June 14, 2005,
   http://news.stanford.edu/news/2005/june15/jobs-061505.html.

Chapter 4: From Orphan to Adopted

1. Unless otherwise noted, all of the statistics in this section are
   quoted or adapted from Wayne Parker, "Statistics on Fatherless
   Children in America," About.com, n.d., http://fatherhood
   .about.com/od/fathersrights/a/fatherless_children.htm.
2. Wayne Parker, "Statistics on Children of Divorce in
   America," About.com, n.d., http://fatherhood.about.com
   /od/fathersrights/a/Statistics-On-Children-Of-Divorce
   -In-America.htm.
3. http://www.onenewsnow.com/Journal/editorial
   .aspx?id=554428. No longer available.

Chapter 6: From Religious to Grace-Covered

1. C. S. Lewis, *The Last Battle* (New York: Collier Books, 1970),
   184; cited in Rick Warren, *The Purpose Driven Life* (Grand
   Rapids: Zondervan, 2002), 39.
2. Frank Viola and Len Sweet, *Jesus: A Theography* (Nashville:
   Thomas Nelson, 2012), 294.
3. Ken Boa, *Conformed to His Image* (Grand Rapids: Zondervan,
   2001), 120.

Chapter 7: From Consumer to Contributor

1. J. P. Moreland, *Kingdom Triangle: Recover the Christian Mind,
   Renovate the Soul, Restore the Spirit's Power* (Grand Rapids:
   Zondervan, 2007), 25.
2. Ibid., 142–43.
3. Skye Jethani, "My Real/Fake Interview on Consumerism: A
   fictional conversation with Pete Tegeler, *Skyebox*,
   July 3, 2009, http://www.skyejethani.com
   /my-realfake-interview-on-consumerism/367/.

4. Ken Boa, *Face to Face: Praying the Scriptures for Intimate Worship* (Grand Rapids: Zondervan, 1997), x.
5. "Our Vision and Values," Transformation Church website, "New Here?" page, http://www.transformationchurch.tc /newhere/visionvalues.php.

Chapter 10: From Failure to Faithful

1. http://www.pocketchanged.com/2012/01/30 /quotes-overcome-fear-of-failure/.
2. Rob Bell, *Velvet Elvis* (Grand Rapids: Zondervan, 2005), 125.
3. Ibid.
4. Ibid., 126.
5. Ibid., 127.
6. Ibid.
7. Ibid., 129.

ABOUT THE AUTHOR

DERWIN L. GRAY IS THE FOUNDING AND LEAD PASTOR OF TRANSFORMATION Church (www.TransformationChurch.tc). He is considered one of America's leading voices on multiethnic, multigenerational, and missional ministry. In its first two years of existence, Transformation Church was recognized as one of the top one hundred fastest-growing churches in America by *Outreach* magazine (second on the list by percentage for 2010).

After graduating from Brigham Young University, Derwin played for six seasons in the NFL for the Indianapolis Colts (1993–1997) and the Carolina Panthers (1998). He graduated magna cum laude, with a master's of divinity with a concentration in apologetics, from Southern Evangelical Seminary, where he was mentored by renowned theologian and philosopher Dr. Norman Geisler. He is also recognized by many as the "Evangelism Linebacker."

Derwin has been married to his best friend, Vicki, for twenty-one years. They have two children, Presley and Jeremiah.

Learn more about Derwin at www.derwinlgray.com.